BRIA

MADE
FOR
MORE

7 PROVEN
STRATEGIES
FOR REACHING
YOUR FULL
POTENTIAL

©2015 by Brian Kinsey

©2015 Dust Jacket Press
Made for More / Brian Kinsey

ISBN: 978-1-943140-43-5

All rights reserved. No part of this publication may be reproduced, distributed, or transmitted in any form or by any means, including photocopying, recording, or other electronic or mechanical methods, without the prior written permission of the publisher, except in the case of brief quotations embodied in critical reviews and certain other noncommercial uses permitted by copyright law. For permission requests, write to the publisher, addressed at the address below:

Dust Jacket Press
P.O. Box 721243
Oklahoma City, OK 73172
www.dustjacket.com

Ordering information for print editions:
Quantity sales. Special discounts are available on quantity purchases by corporations, associations, and others. For details, contact the Dust Jacket Press address above.

Individual sales. Dust Jacket Press publications are available through most bookstores. They can also be ordered directly from Dust Jacket: Tel: (800) 495-0192; Email: info@dustjacket.com; www.dustjacket.com

Dust Jacket logos are registered trademarks of Dust Jacket Press, Inc.

All Scripture quotations, unless otherwise indicated, are taken from THE HOLY BIBLE, KING JAMES VERSION.

Scripture quotations marked " NIV" are taken from the Holy Bible, New International Version® NIV®. Copyright ©1973, 1978, 1984, 2011 by Biblica, Inc. Used by permission of Zondervan. All rights reserved worldwide. www.zondervan.com. The " NIV" and "New International Version" are trademarks registered in the United States Patent and Trademark Office by Biblica, Inc.

Scripture quotations marked (NLT) are taken from the Holy Bible, New Living Translation, copyright © 1996, 2004, 2007 by Tyndale House Foundation. Used by permission of Tyndale House Publishers, Inc., Carol Stream, Illinois 60188. All rights reserved.

Cover & Interior Design: D.E. West / Dust Jacket Creative Services

Printed in the United States of America

www.dustjacket.com

Dedication

To all fellow seekers who, with divine discontent and hungry souls, treasure every opportunity to grow, to seize the moment, and to reach their full potential.

Contents

Acknowledgements vii

Foreword ix

You Were Made for More 1

Before You Begin: Provisions for the Journey 5

Strategy No. 1: Discover Your Purpose 29

Strategy No. 2: Accept Personal Responsibility 47

Strategy No. 3: Take Spiritual Authority 69

Strategy No. 4: Seek Divine Favor 91

Strategy No. 5: Learn from Pain 113

Strategy No. 6: Practice Strategic Thinking 133

Strategy No. 7: Sacrifice Good for Best 157

Completing Your Journey 177

Notes 183

v

Acknowledgements

For almost any author to be successful, it requires a team of contributors who strive to improve and fine-tune a project until it is ready for others to read. This work is no exception. Several people have added their expertise to this project, or to me personally, to enhance and advance the work and make my life better.

I give honor to Alan Fine whose book, *You Already Know How to Be Great*, gave me the faith, fire, and focus to write, to remove the obstacles that hindered my path, and inspired me to reach my full potential. Thank you Alan; not only has your writing motivated me but your friendship and coaching have been truly invaluable.

To my good friend Mark Cole, who, with his diligent and patient coaching, lifted me to a higher level and helped me to strategize for victory. Thank you, Mark, for your friendship and your timeless counsel.

To my wife, Lanette, my companion and proofreader, who worked diligently to make this book its very best and whose unfailing love and devotion to me personally has lifted me to a higher level.

Words cannot describe how much I appreciate Larry Wilson, my editor and fellow writer. Without his exceptional skill this book would never have been possible.

I want to give special honor to Stan Toler, who wrote the Foreword and whose support, coaching, and recommendations have elevated my vision and made it possible for me to reach my potential as a writer.

Thank you all for joining my quest for *More*.

—BRIAN KINSEY

Foreword

As a young boy growing up in rural West Virginia, I had an innate sense that my life had purpose. Life was difficult for our family, especially after my father was killed in a work-related accident when I was just eleven years old. Still, I believed that there was something more for me on this earth. I soon discovered that purpose when I was called to preach at the age of seventeen. Since then I have been blessed by opportunities to proclaim the gospel on six continents, pastor churches in several states, and serve at the highest level of leadership in my denomination. I thank God each day for the growth in my life—growth that has led me to increasingly greater levels of opportunity.

Over the years, however, I have observed that many people never realize their God-given potential. Some seem unaware that they have been created for a higher purpose. Others realize this but become so mired in the concerns of life that they don't make progress or grow. They feel trapped by their circumstances. Still others are simply unable to see a clear path forward. They have a longing for something more, but they don't know how to pursue it.

This book is a treasure for all of those seeking to discover their purpose, reach their potential, and achieve God's best for them. Over the years I have known Brian Kinsey, I've observed him consistently living out the strategies contained within these pages. He is a living testimony of the power of taking simple, consistent steps to discover your purpose and achieve your potential. Here you will find the wisdom, gentle encouragement, and practical strategies that will move you from where you are to a higher level of achievement, contentment, and satisfaction. Your full potential is within your reach! All you have to do is begin the journey.

—STAN TOLER

BRIAN KINSEY

You Were Made for More

*When I was a child, I spake as a child, I understood
as a child, I thought as a child: but when
I became a man, I put away childish things.
—1 Corinthians 13:11*

Every person, regardless of his or her station in life, has the God-given potential to be something more than they currently are. We are all aware of this at some level. We know that God has created us for more—more holiness, more fruitfulness, better relationships, less guilt, fewer regrets. We instinctively know that we have unrealized potential, regardless of how much progress we may already have made. God could do more in us, with us, and through us if we were more fully available to him and more fully saturated with his Holy Spirit.

This truth is not for pastors only. Every believer has the potential to grow, to become more like Christ and more effective in his Kingdom. And it isn't true only of new believers. No matter

1

how long a person has walked with the Lord, he or she has room—and responsibility—to keep seeking, keep growing. Spiritual growth is not a course of study that ends with graduation. You will be growing in Christ for all eternity. And one of the great tragedies of our day is that so many Christians ignore or defer both the need and opportunity to be transformed by the Spirit of God.

You were made for more.

Sadly, even those who are aware of this possibility often pursue growth in the wrong way. Like naïve travelers who set off on a trip to Australia by car, they have a good destination in mind but have chosen the wrong means to get there. It is impossible to grow spiritually simply by doing more. Spiritual transformation does not result from adding more religious practices to your life. Church attendance, tithing, Bible reading, and serving others are wonderful activities. However, piling on religious duties won't make you grow spiritually. You cannot tithe your way to spiritual growth any more than you can ride a bike to the moon. Spiritual practices do support growth, and they certainly result from it; but these things alone will not make you a better person. To be something more, you need something more.

Eight-year-old Robert rode on the church bus to a children's revival. Robert was from a rough neighborhood, neglected by his parents, and in need of more. That night he accepted the invitation to the altar, where he cried like a baby and was filled with the Holy Ghost. When he had finished praying, an altar worker began to explain that what he was feeling was God's love for him. This lost little boy was overwhelmed with the warmth and the joy of God's spirit. He certainly didn't have much in life, and maybe that was what prompted his question to the altar worker: "Can I have as much of this as I want?"

That *more* is a daily, personal, intimate relationship with God. Your desire will determine how far and deep that relationship grows. His presence with you and in you through God's Spirit is the fuel that will power your growth. Spiritual transformation is not something you can accomplish on your own, no matter how successful you may be in other areas of life. This is the work of God. Only he can reshape and refine you, forgiving your past, cleansing your mind and heart in the present, and opening the way to a new future. You don't need more willpower or more muscle power. You need a closer, more vital relationship with your heavenly Father.

That's what this book is about.

I want to help you understand, identify, and remove the barriers to a deeper relationship with God. We grow by our connection to him; therefore, it is essential to understand the things that will enhance that relationship and the things that detract from it.

The busyness of life—even the busyness of church—demands so much of our time and attention that we are not able to keep in close contact with God, overcome sin in our lives, and function the way he wants us to. Ironically, many pastors and other Christian workers spend so much time investing in the kingdom that they fail to pay attention to their own heart. Even the apostle Paul had this concern and warned about it, saying, "But I keep under my body, and bring it into subjection: lest that by any means, when I have preached to others, I myself should be a castaway" (1 Cor. 9:27). I have seen many Christians—even pastors—fall into this trap. Some have even failed morally and walked away from ministry simply because they became too overwhelmed to maintain their spiritual health. Though many have repented, salvaging their marriage and their own salvation, they nevertheless failed to live up to their full potential in Christ.

I want more for you.

I want more for every believer, every pastor, every church volunteer, every follower of Jesus. My aim in writing this book is not merely to build a hospital at the bottom of the hill to help and heal those who have fallen—though I do believe in saving and restoring grace. Rather, I want to build a Temple at the top of the hill, a place of hope, of worship, of intimate fellowship, that will draw all people to a deeper, closer, more powerful relationship with Jesus Christ.

Once there, I want to construct a guardrail—a fence—to ensure that we continue in close fellowship with the Father. We need solid principles and consistent actions that will keep us from sliding back into old habits and practices. This fence has seven sides. They are seven spiritual principles that will open your eyes to weaknesses in your life, make you aware of the *more* that God has for you, and ensure that your relationship with him remains intimate, vibrant, and strong. When we are finished, you will have a clearer picture of what your life could be, and you will have identified practical action steps for moving in that direction. You will be energized, equipped, and motivated to set out on the greatest adventure of your life—reaching your full potential in Christ.

Are you ready?

BRIAN KINSEY

*Before You Begin
Provisions for the Journey*

> *For which of you, intending to build a tower,
> sitteth not down first and counteth the cost,
> whether he have sufficient to finish it?*
> —Luke 14:28

On June 15, 1910, the sailing ship *Terra Nova* set out from Cardiff, Wales, carrying sixty-five men, thirty-four dogs, nineteen Siberian ponies, and three motorized sleds. Their destination: the South Pole. Under the command of veteran Antarctic explorer Robert Falcon Scott, the men of the British Antarctic Expedition, informally known as the Terra Nova Expedition, had the goal to become the first explorers to reach the South Pole. After a year and a half of preparation, including preliminary expeditions to stage supplies along the polar route, Scott and four others finally arrived at the pole on January 17, 1912—only to find a Norwegian flag, planted there by rival explorer Roald Amundsen just thirty-one days earlier.

Scott and his men were undaunted, however, because their expedition had more than one objective. The party had planned also to conduct scientific and geographical research, including a study of the penguin colony at Cape Crozier, and the exploration of a region known as King Edward VII Land. Prior to the trip, the team's chief scientist, Edward Wilson, had stated that the primary aim of the expedition was scientific discovery. He wrote to a friend, "No one can say that it will have only been a Pole-hunt . . . We want the scientific work to make the bagging of the Pole merely an item in the results."[1] Indeed, on their return journey, Scott's party did find fossilized plants, proving that Antarctica had once been wooded and joined to other continents.[2]

Yet today, Robert Scott and the Terra Nova Expedition are known neither for reaching the South Pole nor for discovering evidence of forestation on Antarctica. They are known for tragic failure. The return journey of Scott and his companions was marked by a series of poor decisions and misfortunes. One crewmember, severely frostbitten and suffering from a head injury, collapsed and died on February 17.[3] Having missed a rendezvous with a resupply team, Scott's group grew critically low on supplies. Thirty days later a second crewmember, both hands and feet useless from frostbite, told his companions, "I am just going outside and may be some time."[4] He left the tent and abandoned himself to an icy death.

A fierce blizzard commenced on March 20, with temperatures reaching -44 degrees Fahrenheit. Nine days later, Scott made this final entry in his journal: "We shall stick it out to the end, but we are getting weaker, of course, and the end cannot be far. It seems a pity but I do not think I can write more— R. Scott. Last entry—For God's sake look after our people."[5] Eight months later a search party discovered his frozen body along with those of his remaining crewmembers, just eleven miles from their next supply depot. All had perished from a combination of exhaustion, starvation, and hypothermia.

In the century since the Terra Nova expedition, researchers have studied the causes of the disaster. While many see Scott as a tragic hero, others view him as a well-meaning bungler whose mission was doomed from the start. Unlike Amundsen, whose expedition had a single focus—the race to the pole—Scott undertook at least three aims: polar discovery, scientific research, and geographical exploration. Where Amundsen relied wholly on sled dogs for transportation, Scott experimented with ponies and mechanized sleds, both of which proved wholly inadequate for the harsh conditions. The group was undersupplied and chronically short of fuel. Scholars may debate the precise reasons for Scott's failure, but the supreme lesson from this heartbreaking story is clear: to accomplish your goal, you must have a clear objective, and you must be adequately prepared for the journey.

DESTINATION: YOUR FULL POTENTIAL

Few people ever reach their full potential. As with the Terra Nova Expedition, there may be many underlying causes for this, though chief among them is that most people never set out with that goal in mind. They never intend to reach their full potential. Or, they may have a vague aspiration to grow in Christ, to achieve all that he intends for them, but are so distracted by competing aims that they never zero in with single-minded determination, as Roald Amundsen did, on one, clear objective. These leaders are like the seed that fell on thorny ground in Jesus' parable of the sower. Jesus said, "The seed falling among the thorns refers to someone who hears the word, but the worries of this life and the deceitfulness of wealth choke the word, making it unfruitful" (Matt. 13:22 NIV).

REASONS WE FALL SHORT

For many people, and especially church leaders, those worries of life can take the form of church itself. It is possible to become so wrapped up in the work of ministry, helping others grow to their full potential, that you neglect your own growth. And there are many other side roads that may run parallel to God's plan but do not lead to a life of holiness and fruitfulness. Success in business, enjoying the rewards of hard work, devoting energy to a family, pursuing education, travel: all these are good things. Yet they can make a person unfruitful to the extent that they distract from reaching for the full blessing God has in store for each of us.

Personal hurts are another serious threat to reaching your full potential. Each of us has personal wounds from broken relationships, wrongs done to us, grief, or other hardships we have experienced. Like the storms encountered by polar explorers, these personal hurts can be unpredictable and devastating. Any one of them may derail you from seeking God's highest calling for your life. Revenge, self-pity, seeking to build your self-esteem through illegitimate means such as illicit sexuality, materialism, substance abuse, or controlling behavior also can pull your focus away from God and his best. There are any number of things that may divide your energy, leading you to fall short of your full potential.

Now think of the single-minded ambition of the apostle Paul to lay hold of God's best for himself. Paul wrote:

> *Not as though I had already attained, either were already perfect: but I follow after, if that I may apprehend that for which also I am apprehended of Christ Jesus. Brethren, I count not myself to have apprehended: but this one thing I do, forgetting those things which are behind, and reaching forth unto those things which are before, I press toward the mark for the prize of the high calling of God in Christ Jesus. (Phil. 3:12–14)*

Paul was determined to reach his full potential in Christ. This was his single-minded obsession: to become all that God wanted him to be!

YOU HAVE POTENTIAL

Perhaps you struggle to believe that more is possible for your life. Many people, especially those who have experienced setbacks or failure in the past, simply give up on the idea that further growth is possible. Having stopped short of graduation, you may think it impossible that you could ever earn a degree or improve your mind. Having failed morally, especially if that failure has been repeated, you may conclude, "That's just who I am." If you have had setbacks in your marriage or your ministry, you may settle into the idea that "this is as good as it gets."

Yet no matter where you are in life—or where you have been—you have the potential to become the person God has always intended you to be. The writer of Proverbs says, "There is surely a future hope for you, and your hope will not be cut off" (23:18 NIV). With God, the future is always better than the past. You—yes, you—have great potential!

POTENTIAL FRUITFULNESS

Do you know what your full potential is? Can you visualize it? What would it look like if you were to reach your potential in Christ? Many people have no idea what their full potential is—or even what direction to look for it. To reach your destination, you must first know what that destination is.

Simply put, growth is fruit. Growing to your full potential will mean producing more fruit in your life. Jesus said, "Ye have not chosen me, but I have chosen you, and ordained you, that ye should go and bring forth fruit, and that your fruit should remain: that whatsoever ye shall ask of the Father in my name, he may give it you" (John 15:16). Paul defined fruitfulness this way: "But the fruit of the Spirit is love, joy, peace, longsuffering, gentleness, goodness, faith, meekness, temperance: against such there is no law" (Gal. 5:22–23). And Jesus clearly tells us the means to achieving this fruitful life: "I am the vine, ye are the branches: He that abideth in me, and I in him, the same bringeth forth much fruit: for without me ye can do nothing" (John 15:5).

You will grow to your full potential by abiding in Christ: staying close to him, living in an intimate fellowship with him. You will not reach your full potential by going it alone, by trying harder, by using self-help techniques or the latest fads in psychology or ministry. Your life can be fully transformed only through a close relationship with Christ through the Holy Spirit. Nothing else will get you there.

And the result will be fruitfulness in your life and ministry. What does your full potential look like? It looks like a person who is joyful, faithful, self-disciplined, loving, patient, and kind. It looks like you, transformed by the power of the Holy Ghost. And it results in effective ministry to others. Jesus said that those who remain in this close fellowship with him may ask for anything in his name. What would you ask for in your ministry, your family, the Kingdom? What mission might God entrust to you as you grow in fruitfulness? What impact might you have on your church, your community—on the world?

Can you imagine your full potential? Can you picture what your life would be like if you were finally, fully transformed by the Holy Ghost?

IN PURSUIT OF THE GOAL

Have you made the decision to grow in Christ? Have you determined, like Paul, that you will allow no distractions, no impediments, nothing to stop you from obtaining the prize of the high calling of God in Christ Jesus? You cannot hope to reach your full potential without this resolve.

You may have made such resolves in the past but failed to keep them. It is possible that you have "laid it all on the altar" before, only to allow the worries and cares of life distract you from seeking God's best. It is time to put those failures in the past. As believers in Jesus Christ, and especially as leaders of his church, we must focus on our growth and not on our past failures. We all fail at times, and you may fail again in the future. Resolve to "fail forward," as John C. Maxwell has put it, accepting God's forgiveness, learning from your mistakes, and using that knowledge to further your growth. Remember, "there is therefore now no condemnation to them which are in Christ Jesus, who walk not after the flesh, but after the Spirit" (Rom. 8:1). God does not chain us to the past; he frees us for the future. The book of Revelation says that the fearful have no hope (see 21:8). You cannot reach your full potential while burdened by fears, regrets, guilt, or insecurity. Do not allow such things to prevent you from setting out on this journey with Christ. Be at peace. Listen to the One who speaks peace to you. Seek the prize, the high calling of God in Christ Jesus. And to do that, you must adequately prepare for the journey.

PROVISIONS FOR THE JOURNEY

The Terra Nova expedition failed in part because it had a divided focus. Now that you have a single-minded passion to achieve God's best for yourself, you have the first prerequisite for success: a clear goal. But you need more. Robert Scott and his men might have succeeded in spite of the distraction of other research had they been properly supplied. They lacked adequate food and fuel, two basic necessities for any journey. In the same way, you will need the provisions that will sustain you when the journey becomes long and difficult. Growth is a lifelong journey and you will need to create a strategy for it. There are five basic things you will need each day to reach your full potential. They are:

- Purpose
- Hope
- Encouragement
- A Positive Attitude
- Determination

PURPOSE

Many people never realize their full potential in Christ because they have not discovered their one purpose, or calling, in life. God has called and gifted you uniquely. You don't have to be a pastor or work full-time in ministry to have a role in God's Kingdom. God calls everyone to serve. The apostle Paul put it this way in his letter to the church in Ephesus:

> *But unto every one of us is given grace according to the measure of the gift of Christ. Wherefore he saith, When he ascended up on high, he led captivity captive, and gave gifts unto men . . . And he gave some, apostles; and some, prophets; and some, evangelists; and some, pastors and teachers; For the perfecting of the saints, for the work of the ministry, for the edifying of the body of Christ." (Eph. 4:7–8, 11–12)*

Make no mistake; you *do* have a purpose. Seek that purpose through prayer. This is how you will come to understand the will of God for your life. If you are not praying daily, you are not walking with God. Ask the Holy Spirit to reveal his will to you. Seek the gifting that the Spirit will give you. You have a role to play in the body of Christ, helping others to reach their full potential also. When trying to determine God's plan for you, be patient and wait on the Lord. During that time of waiting, encourage yourself and learn to speak hope to others as well.

When you have discovered the purpose that God has for you, write it down. Tell others about it. Put it somewhere you will see it frequently, such as on your refrigerator, inside your Bible, or on your desk. When the going gets tough, remember why you are on this journey: God has called you to a purpose. Visualize the difference you will make in your family, in the church, and in the world if you keep going. Remembering *why* this matters will keep you motivated.

To keep this focus, learn to heed the warnings when God rebukes you. He will do that occasionally, correcting you to keep you on track. You will feel this through the convicting power of the

Holy Ghost, warning you of hidden sins or of attitudes or actions that lead you in the wrong direction. You may occasionally receive this kind of admonition through the wise counsel or criticism of godly people. Rejoice when you are chastised in this way, and don't grieve over it. Remember that if you have to be rebuked by your pastor or another saint, you have not listened to the warnings of the Lord. He will always try to chasten you first. That chastening proves that you are a child of God. Remain focused on your purpose, and do not be discouraged. You can become better tomorrow than you are today. As a Spanish proverb says, "He who does not look ahead remains behind." Learn to cast hope for the future in everything you do and say.

HOPE

The second daily provision that you will need on your journey to full potential is hope. Here at the beginning, your emotions and enthusiasm will run high. You are at the start of a journey that will take you to places you have not yet imagined—both spiritually and in your ministry. But it will be a long journey, and you are sure to face setbacks. Among the most difficult tests to endure is the persistent feeling that you will never reach your goal, that your heart and life cannot change but will always be exactly as you are today. That thinking will defeat you if it goes unchecked. To counter it, you need one of the greatest of all spiritual blessings as your daily food: hope.

Get Hope. Marshal Ferdinand Foch was a hero in the Battle of Verdun during one of the bloodiest and most desperate conflicts of the last century, World War I. The great general is reported to have said, "There are no hopeless situations; there are only men who have grown hopeless about them." You must first acquire and hold on to hope for yourself and for your future. That hope comes from knowledge of God's Word and the ultimate victory of Christ. Call this to mind, and you will have hope no matter how bleak your circumstances may seem. Remember, there is no power in fear. Revelation 21:8 states: "But the fearful, and unbelieving, and the abominable, and murderers, and whoremongers, and sorcerers, and idolaters, and all liars, shall have their part in the lake which burneth with fire and brimstone: which is the second death." The fearful have no hope. Resist the negative thinking that leads to self-pity and despair. Remember that hope is not spiritually given; it's purposefully driven. Choose faith. Choose hope. Do not allow circumstances to overwhelm you. A quotation attributed to Dr. Martin Luther King Jr. says, "We must accept finite disappointment but never lose ultimate hope." Situations are never hopeless. It is your perspective on the situation that determines whether you will be hopeful or hopeless.

Begin your journey with hope of a good outcome, and reinforce that hope each day by meditating on the Word and choosing positive responses to your emotions and circumstances. You will finish this journey the way you began it. If you do not begin with hope, you will not acquire it along the way. Start with hope.

Give Hope. Winston Churchill was once asked by a reporter what was his country's greatest weapon in fighting against Hitler's Nazi regime. Reportedly, Churchill responded without a moment's hesitation: "It was what England's greatest weapon has always been—hope." Be a bringer of hope to others. As you do, you will help both them and yourself reach your full potential. Many people lack the hopeful outlook that would enable them to rise above their circumstances and seek God's best. Either they do not know the promises of God or else they have been so overwhelmed by their negative circumstances that they have lost sight of hope. To strengthen both them and yourself, impart the message of hope to those around you. Beware of dwelling too long with negative thinkers or those who lack hope. Direct their attention to the Word of God and to the ultimate victory of Christ. Help others rise above negativism and despair, and it will speed you on your own journey. People need hope. Speak hope, and you will keep hope.

ENCOURAGEMENT

King David was one of the most hopeful and purposeful of all leaders in God's Kingdom. His exploits are the stuff of legend. Yet he was human, and he was subject to discouragement. If even David suffered from grief, heartache, and discouragement, how much more will you and I be subject to these things? The journey to reach your full potential will take longer than you think and be more difficult than you would like.

On one occasion, David and his fighting men returned home to find the village where they stayed had been destroyed and all of their families taken captive. It was a desperate time. David himself was "greatly distressed." What's more, his own men talked openly about stoning him "because the soul of all the people was grieved, every man for his sons and for his daughters." That's when David did something you must certainly learn to do on your journey: "David encouraged himself in the LORD his God" (1 Sam. 30:6).

Encouragement is not only a gift others give to you. It is an activity that you must practice. Just as eating properly fuels your body and regular exercise keeps you in good physical condition, so the consistent practice of encouragement will keep you spiritually fit, hopeful, and living on purpose. Here are some simple ways to do that.

Pray in the Holy Ghost. To encourage yourself in the Lord, you must learn the principle of Jude 20: "But ye, beloved, building up yourselves on your most holy faith, praying in the Holy Ghost." God cannot—will not—change you if you do not purposefully pray in the Holy Ghost. Through prayer, enter the Holy of Holies and learn to worship God there. Worship in your heart when the church comes together, even before the service begins or the music starts. Pray in the Spirit, and become aware of those praying around you; when you connect with others and come into agreement together it increases your opportunity to become more than you are now. When Jesus said "Lift up your eyes" (John 4:35), he was speaking about cultivating awareness. When you do, you will recognize the harvest standing all around you and be strengthened by the fellowship of brothers and sisters in prayer. Break out of the box, and pray with those who are seeking along with you. Your heart will be encouraged, and you will grow.

Wait on the Lord. To avoid impulsive thinking, train yourself to wait on the Lord. Jesus displayed uncommon calmness during his ministry, and though he faced many tense situations, he never panicked. Encouragement comes from choosing patience over anxiety, restraint over impulse. Rest assured that God will speak. God will move. God will cause you to grow. And that will happen on his timetable, not yours. Learn to relax, find joy in the journey, and trust that God's ultimate plan for your life will be accomplished. Impulsive people speak before they think. They are in a rush to find an instant solution to every situation, and that often ends in disaster. To avoid this impulse, acquire the discipline of waiting on the Lord. Listen to the words of Oswald Chambers:

> *Impulsiveness is all right in a child, but it is disastrous in a man or woman—an impulsive adult is always a spoiled person. Impulsiveness needs to be trained into intuition by discipline.*
>
> *Discipleship is built entirely on the supernatural grace of God. Walking on water is easy to someone with impulsive boldness, but walking on dry land as a disciple of Jesus Christ is something altogether different. Peter walked on the water to go to Jesus, but he "followed him at a distance" on dry land (Mark 14:54). We do not need the grace of God to withstand crises—human nature and pride are sufficient for us to face the stress and strain magnificently. But it does require the supernatural grace of God to live twenty-four hours a day as a saint, going through drudgery and living an ordinary, unnoticed, and ignored existence as a disciple of Jesus. It is ingrained in us that we have to do exceptional things for God—but we do not. We have to be exceptional in the ordinary things of life, and holy on the ordinary streets, among ordinary people—and this is not learned in five minutes.*[6]

The only reason situations look hopeless is that we feel hopeless. God is still able to do his work, which is beyond our limitations. Just because we are limited does not mean we are without resources. Build yourself up on your most holy faith.

Receive Encouragement from Others. When you are on a path of growth, you will shake hell when you worship and pray with others. Go to church not only to be ministered to but also to minister. Give and receive encouragement with your fellow travelers. Allow others to speak words of grace, hope, and support to you. Surround yourself with positive voices of faith and listen to them.

A POSITIVE ATTITUDE

A fourth daily provision for your journey to full potential is a positive attitude. The Proverbs tell us about the power of a person's attitude, saying, "For as he thinketh in his heart, so is he" (23:7). The thoughts you choose to allow to dwell in your mind will shape you either positively or negatively. On a journey as long and difficult as the road to full potential, you cannot allow a negative attitude to weigh you down. You must feed yourself daily through positive thinking. I don't mean mere humanistic reasoning or shallow, happy talk. I am referring to a positive outlook, based on the truth of God's Word, which forms a foundation for healthy thinking, emotions, and actions. Here are some ways to get and keep a positive attitude.

Eliminate Negative Speech. You have within yourself the single greatest attitude maker or breaker that exists: your own words. The apostle Paul realized this when he wrote: "Do everything without grumbling or arguing, so that you may become blameless and pure, 'children of God without fault in a warped and crooked generation.' Then you will shine among them like stars in the sky as you hold firmly to the word of life" (Phil. 2:14–16 NIV). What you say has a tremendous effect on your attitude and the attitude of others.

Think of the way we often talk ourselves out of doing good things by the way we express our thoughts. You might find yourself saying things like "I don't have time to read the Bible this morning" or "I'm too tired to meet with my small group." Now imagine what a difference it would make if you changed your vocabulary and said, "I get to read my Bible today," or "What a privilege it is to have a group of believers and to encourage each other."

Here are a few simple ways to change your attitude by changing the way you speak. First, eliminate the word *try* from your vocabulary and instead use the word *do*. When someone asks you for a favor, don't say, "I'll try." If you intend to help, say, "Yes, I'll do that." Second, begin using the phrase *get to* rather than *have to*. Don't say, "I have to mow the lawn today." Instead say, "I get to take care of this beautiful home by mowing the lawn." You'll notice yourself becoming more thankful and appreciative of the opportunities you have, and that's the basis for a great attitude.

Also, remove all arguing and complaining from your conversations. You won't grow until you begin to speak in faith, and you can't do that while complaining about your circumstances or about others. Whenever you feel cantankerous, stop and pay attention to what is happening. What makes you feel that way? What are you responding to? From what part of your spirit does this attitude originate? Conquer that attitude through prayer and fasting. Speak your way to freedom by declaring the positive truths of the Word of God. Don't allow yourself to persist in negative attitudes or negative speech.

The writer of Proverbs teaches us that "by the blessing of the upright the city is exalted: but it is overthrown by the mouth of the wicked" (11:11). Your negative words do tremendous damage to yourself and others, but good, pleasing, wholesome words give hope. Again, the Proverbs teach us, "Pleasant words are as an honeycomb, sweet to the soul, and health to the bones" (16:24). And the apostle Paul wrote: "Let no corrupt communication proceed out of your mouth, but that which is good to the use of edifying, that it may minister grace unto the hearers" (Eph. 4:29).

Always speak hope to others. Do not allow naysayers or complainers to set the tone for your conversations and thinking. Avoid complaining because it sucks the life from you and others. Seek solutions rather than dwelling on problems. When you must correct others or point out something negative, use the "sandwich method." Begin with positive words, then discuss the negative observation, and end with words of hope. Do not allow a negative thought to be your last word on any situation. Maintaining hope comes from seeing the potential in every circumstance and remaining positive despite the conditions. Speak hope and you will keep hope.

Commit to Continual Improvement. At the close of World War II, American business and military leaders attempting to help the Japanese rebuild their country introduced the concept of continuous improvement. This concept came to be called *kaizen*, a Chinese and Japanese word meaning "change for better." Kaizen is now a recognized practice in the fields of industry, government, banking, even healthcare. To get and keep a positive attitude, commit yourself to the process of continual improvement.

It has been said that our potential is God's gift to us, and what we do with it is our gift to him. Oftentimes our potential goes unreached because we try to do everything instead of what we are best at. As has so often been said, "Keep the main thing the main thing." Reaching your potential requires focus and a willingness to continue learning, changing, and growing. You can improve a little each day. As you recognize improvement in yourself, celebrate it. Keep growing; keep moving forward.

Forget the Past. Pastor Jack Hayford, chancellor of The King's

University and founding pastor of The Church on the Way in Van Nuys, California, said, "The past is a dead issue, and we can't gain any momentum moving toward tomorrow if we are dragging the past behind us."[7] He might have been thinking of Paul's words in Philippians 3:13–14: "Forgetting those things which are behind, and reaching forth unto those things which are before, I press toward the mark for the prize of the high calling of God in Christ Jesus." To keep a positive attitude, you must not dwell on the past with its mistakes, failures, and disappointments. Rise above them, put them behind you, and keep moving forward. Failure is not final. Keep your purpose before you, and don't look back.

DETERMINATION

Achievement in life is always connected to determination. That is especially true when it comes to reaching your full potential. Olympic records are continually broken through the determination of athletes who are challenged to be their best. Obviously, we need the empowerment of the Holy Spirit in order to reach our full potential as people made in the image of God. This is not a purely human endeavor. Yet you must be a participant in this process. God will do the work of changing your heart only as you yield yourself to him and cooperate with his Holy Spirit. It will not be easy or quick. Reaching your full potential is the work of a lifetime. You will need tremendous focus and determination to reach this goal.

Make determination one of your daily provisions, and it will help you push through when the goal seems too distant or unattainable. Determination has the power to remove restrictions and overcome resistance, to ignite your fire, increase your faith, and give you clarity of focus. It is a key to growth. It is critical that you hunger for growth to the point that *nothing* will discourage you from seeking it. The devil has a way of hitting us at our most vulnerable point to intimidate or discourage us. Determination helps us to persevere. Satan also attacks at our strongest points, trying to convince us that we are wrong, that we don't know what we are doing, that we are incompetent to minister in Jesus' name, that we should simply quit. Determination provides the endurance and courage to recognize the devil's schemes, overcome that resistance, push through the obstacles, and keep going.

We all feel a natural resistance to change and to growth, and sooner or later you will meet resistance from a most unlikely source: yourself. The old you—the person guided by the flesh—will push back against the changes the Spirit is trying to make within you. However, the determined soul continues to work until the job is done. Determination is not an emotional response; it is a decision. Ask God to give you the desire and determination to continue even when everything seems against you. Stop working in the flesh and work in the Spirit.

Determination is easier to develop when you take one step at a time. Progress is measured step by step, day by day, and moment by moment. If you focus on how far you are from your full potential and how many obstacles are before you, you are more likely to quit. Try looking only at today. Think about the next right step, then take it. By taking it one step at a time, you will be more likely to keep going.

Persevere in this journey. Many people give up just before they were about to have a breakthrough. The difference between those who reach their full potential and those who don't is never a matter of talent or skill or natural giftedness. We all have a different level of potential, and one is not better or worse than the next. No, the difference between those who succeed in reaching their full potential and those who languish in the land of "if only" is that those who achieve are willing to keep going just a little bit longer. Don't stop short. Be determined to reach your goal.

Determination produces personal discipline, and you need discipline to reach your full potential. You don't grow automatically when the Holy Ghost comes into your life. You have to "work out your own salvation with fear and trembling. For it is God which worketh in you both to will and to do of his good pleasure" (Phil. 2:12–13). A daily routine of personal spiritual disciplines is absolutely necessary to become everything God wants you to be.

Without resistance, you will not grow. Winston Churchill reportedly said, "Kites rise highest against the wind, not with it." In the same way, it is the resistance of the wind that creates lift under the wings of an airplane. Without resistance, there could be no flight. If being a champion were an easy task, everyone would be wearing gold. Determination is required to reach God's best for you.

Maintain your determination by reinforcing your will with positive talk. Don't talk yourself down; rather, talk up the possibilities in Christ. Learn to speak to yourself and about yourself in a proper way. This is not mere positive self-talk but Word self-talk. When you are facing resistance, especially resistance within yourself, speak the Word over that area of your life. Speak the Word with authority. Claim the promises of God.

The prophet Isaiah wrote, "Because the Sovereign Lord helps me, I will not be disgraced. Therefore, I have set my face like a stone, determined to do his will" (Isa. 50:7, NLT). Are you determined to keep pushing forward, to reach out for your full potential in Christ? I believe you will do it.

THE ROAD FROM HERE

You were made for more, and the remainder of this book is devoted to helping you grow to your full potential as a child of God. Over the next seven chapters, we will learn seven proven strategies that will enable you to reach your full potential. You will see biblical and contemporary examples of those strategies at work. You will gain a vision for what your life might be after the Spirit has done his work in you. And you will be equipped with helpful, practical steps for implementing these strategies in your life. Your life is about to change for the better. Are you ready?

Before diving into the next chapter, I suggest that you take time to do three important things.

BEGIN SEEKING

The journey to reach your full potential is a spiritual one, and you will not succeed on your own. You must be guided by the Spirit and be in daily contact with him. Take time now to pray about the road ahead. Seek God's purpose for yourself. Ask for the Spirit's equipping with purpose, hope, encouragement, positive attitude, and determination. Commit yourself fully to God and fully to this journey of growth.

BEGIN SHARING

The Proverbs tell us, "As iron sharpens iron, so one person sharpens another" (27:17 NIV). You will get further faster on this journey if you share it with one or more people. Right now, write down the names of five people that you might tell about your desire to reach your full potential in Christ. Then invite them to join you on the journey. As you read this book together and talk about how to enact these strategies in your lives, you will bless one another with hope, encouragement, and determination. Consider beginning a mentoring group or small group based around the concepts of this book. Bring others with you on the journey to growth.

BEGIN SAYING

I knew that I had been called to preach at a very young age. When I was only nineteen, the Lord let me know that if I was going to make it as an evangelist, I needed to learn the principle of reinforcing my calling with basic spiritual disciplines repeated daily. I observed the power of going back to basics in the life of Mordecai, cousin to Queen Esther. Mordecai was a man of humble circumstances, but he was greatly honored by the king for his role for uncovering a plot against the king's life (see Esther 6:1–11). At the time, Mordecai was holding a prayer vigil in sackcloth and ashes because of a plot underway against the Jewish people. After the king, grateful for Mordecai's earlier role in saving his life, threw a parade in Mordecai's honor, he "came again to the king's gate" (6:12). He put on sackcloth and continued his prayer vigil, even though he experienced momentary victory and honor. This deliberate, consistent practice of humility and prayer brought the ultimate victory.

Based on that principle, I developed the practice that I have come to call the *Rule of Five*. Though the term itself was coined by John C. Maxwell, I have been practicing this principle for nearly thirty years. As Mordecai returned to the king's gate after a brief victory, I return daily, no matter the circumstances, to these five spiritual practices.

1. Read, study, and pray the Word.

2. Write and teach what I have learned.
3. Share vision to influence a leader.
4. Speak the Word to a hurting heart.
5. Reflect on the day's events.

Choose a Rule of Five for yourself and practice it consistently. Your five actions don't have to be the same as mine. They might be Bible reading, physical exercise, positive thinking, conversation, journaling, prayer, or any number of other growth-related activities. Establish your Rule of Five and do them every single day—including weekends, holidays, and the days you just don't feel like doing anything.

Along with that, take the time now to establish two other *fives*. List five things you would do if you had unlimited resources. This will get you thinking about your full potential—and about what your purpose in life may be. Also, list five scriptures to pray over yourself every day. Consider making this one of the items in your Rule of Five. Put God's Word into your mind every day, and you will be filled with hope, encouraged, and more determined than ever to reach your full potential.

I believe in you. Let's take this journey together!

ACTION LIST

1. Pray for God's leading as you begin to explore your full potential.
2. List the names of five people who could become partners with you on this journey.
3. Establish your Rule of Five—the five positive activities that you will do each day.
4. List five things you would do if you had unlimited

resources, and the five scriptures you will pray over yourself daily.

5. Share your excitement over beginning this journey with someone else.

STRATEGY NO. 1

Discover Your Purpose

All Growth Is Intentional

> *Be very careful, then, how you live—not as unwise but as wise, making the most of every opportunity, because the days are evil.*
> —*Ephesians 5:15–16* NIV

Billy Graham is the best known and probably the most successful evangelist of the modern era. Born in 1918, Graham rose to prominence during the 1940s and '50s through large, citywide campaigns where he proclaimed the gospel to thousands at a time. Graham held evangelistic meetings in London that lasted for twelve weeks, and a 1957 campaign in New York City that ran nightly for sixteen weeks, allowing some 2.3 million people to hear the gospel. All together, Billy Graham has conducted more than four hundred evangelistic campaigns in 185 countries and territories on six continents. Many of Billy Graham's rallies were broadcast on television, and his *Hour of Decision* radio program aired for some fifty years. His estimated lifetime audience, including live events and mass media, is likely over 2.2 billion.

How does a person achieve such fruitfulness in ministry? Is it luck? Being in the right place at the right time? Certainly, God's plan and provision were essential to Dr. Graham's ministry—and to the success of any gospel endeavor. Yet another factor also contributed to the evangelist's incredible productivity: his intentionality, his sense of purpose, his unwavering focus on the work to which God had called him.

It is reported that NBC once offered Billy Graham a five-year contract for one million dollars to appear on television opposite popular CBS television host Arthur Godfrey. Graham turned down the offer so he could continue holding evangelistic rallies. And his passion for sharing the gospel went beyond mass evangelism; he found a way to offer the good news in virtually every conversation. A. Larry Ross, who handled media and public relations for Billy Graham for more than twenty years, quipped, "You can ask Billy Graham how he gets his suits dry-cleaned on the road, and he'll turn it into a gospel witness." Prior to television interviews, when technicians ask the guest to do a sound microphone check, most recite the alphabet or make a comment about the weather. But not Billy Graham. According to Ross, Graham always recited John 3:16: "For God so loved the world, that he gave his only begotten Son, that whosoever believeth in him should not perish, but have everlasting life." When Ross asked the evangelist about it, Graham said, "Because that way, if I am not able to communicate the gospel clearly during the interview, at least the cameraman will have heard it."[1] Everything he did was focused on his life's one great purpose.

You don't achieve a seventy-year ministry by accident. That

kind of potential is realized only through sustained, purposeful effort. I have always admired Billy Graham for his lifetime of faithful service, lived without a hint of the scandal or controversy that has plagued many in the public eye. He lived his life on purpose.

And that brings us to Strategy No. 1 for reaching your full potential: *Discover Your Purpose*. Simply stated, all growth is intentional. To reach your full potential, you will need more than good wishes, more than the encouragement of others, and even more than God's blessing—vital as that is. You need a sustained, intentional approach to achieving all that God has in store for you. You need both a *purpose* and *purposefulness*. Growth does not happen by chance or luck. You must intentionally pursue it.

Let's explore this strategy by understanding four key ideas:

- The Fallacy of Time
- The Power of Vision
- The Brutal Facts
- The Internal Engine

Then we will examine some practical steps for putting this strategy into action. At the conclusion of this chapter, you will understand the power of discovering your purpose and have a clear action plan for being proactive in your pursuit of full potential.

THE FALLACY OF TIME

Growth takes time, but time does not produce growth.

Most people are convinced that time is their great ally in the pursuit of growth. Good things take time, we often say. Without realizing it, many have accepted the idea that the mere passage of time will bring the positive changes they seek. That simply is not true. Yes, time is an element in the process of growth and healing. When you are ill or injured, God's healing work in your body may be seen over time. You may often hear that advice from your doctor: "Just give it some time." And we see that children grow over time. A healthy two year old will be larger than a newborn, and a twenty-one year old will have matured in many ways.

However, age alone does not make a person mature. Wisdom, life skills, the ability to live independently—all that we call maturity—doesn't come simply by waiting for eighteen years. A child must be taught, disciplined, and trained in order to become an adult. In the same way, time alone does not heal wounds—physical, spiritual, or emotional. Healing may take time, but time is not the agent of healing. Physical recovery requires nutrition, rest, medicines, and therapy. Spiritual healing requires confession, repentance, and forgiveness. Emotional healing depends on self-awareness, communication, and acceptance. Add five years to the life of a bitter, cantankerous person, and you simply have an older grouch. Spiritual growth requires action—consistent, purposeful action. Waiting longer will not solve the problems in your life. You must do something.

Jesus illustrated that principle in his parable of the talents (see Matt. 25:14–30). According to the story, a man went on a journey and entrusted three servants with a different amount of money: five talents, two talents, and one talent, each according to their potential. When the man returned, he was pleased to find that the servants who had been given five and two talents had each doubled their money through wise investments. The servant with just one talent, however, had dug a hole and buried the money.

He did nothing, gained nothing, and earned a severe reprimand from his master. You cannot bury your potential in the ground and expect it to grow. You must do something with it.

Too many people don't realize their full potential because their desire for growth is nothing more than a wish. They see the need to grow, and even desire it. But they are unwilling to put forth the effort to make it happen. They wrongly believe that time alone will bring them to maturity. Don't make that mistake. Do not mistake your awareness of the need for action for action itself. Do not fall for the idea that waiting another month or another year will somehow make you more disciplined or cause you to reach your potential. Those who are eager to improve their lives but unwilling to change will remain forever the same. If all you are willing to do is what you are doing, then all you will ever be is what you are. To realize your full potential, you must be purposeful about it.

THE POWER OF VISION

You must have a compelling vision for your life in order to grow.

All change is driven by one of two forces: pain or passion. It is possible that the first factor is driving you to seek change now. Some circumstance in your life has become so painful that you realize change must come. Perhaps you are so stressed about your work that you are unable to sleep. Or you may have difficulty in your marriage or family, or perhaps you are being crushed by a burden of debt. The pain of that circumstance, whatever it is, has led you to the point of change. And that is a valid starting point. Pain, more broadly defined as negative circumstances, has sparked many a reform and revolution. When the pain of remaining the same becomes too great, people seek change.

However, passion is a much stronger and longer lasting motivator for change. To reach your full potential in Christ, you must eventually move beyond responding to pain to pursuing a powerful vision for your life. This vision will become the passion that both drives and sustains you. Remember the example of Billy Graham. It was his passion for evangelism and positive vision, not a desire to create better personal circumstances, that fueled his ministry for some seventy years.

Few people have achieved more of their personal potential than Joseph, son of the patriarch Jacob. As a boy, Joseph had a series of dreams in which God revealed Joseph's potential to him. Though he didn't fully understand the dreams, it seemed clear that he would eventually be in a position of authority over his ten older brothers, something highly unlikely in that ancient culture. Joseph made the mistake of telling his brothers about the dreams, and they hated him for it. In a fit of jealousy, they sold "the dreamer" into slavery and tricked their father into believing he was dead (see Genesis 37 and following for the entire story). Joseph held onto the dream, however. He knew he was destined for greatness, and that belief guided him, first as the head of Potiphar's household, later as a prisoner unjustly accused, and finally as prime minister of Egypt. Joseph remained true to God's vision for his life, and those childhood dreams did come true. His ten older brothers bowed before him, placing their lives in the hands of the brother they had once despised. Joseph's unwavering faithfulness to God's vision for his life had placed him in a position to bless his entire family.

What is your vision for your life? What do you hope to be, by God's grace? What has God revealed to you about your potential? Is it winning souls? Is it preaching the Word? Is it teaching children, or governing wisely, or healing others? "'For I know the plans I have for you,' declares the LORD, 'plans to prosper you and not to harm you, plans to give you hope and a future'" (Jer. 29:11 NIV). God does have a purpose in mind for you, as we learned in the previous chapter. Have you discovered that purpose yet? If not, pray diligently on the matter. Ask God to reveal himself. Ask the advice of trusted friends who can assess your spiritual gifts and natural abilities. When you discover this passion, it will point you forward toward your full potential. Every person needs this internal compass to guide them on the journey.

Like Joseph, you will have critics and detractors. There will always be someone working against you as you press toward your vision because as you fulfill your calling, they will feel convicted about their own life. You must learn to lovingly ignore these critics and focus instead on the audience that truly matters—God. Don't let naysayers or detractors sap your motivation. Believe that your vision is from God, and take responsibility for pursuing it. Don't become discouraged; keep doing the right things and your emotions will follow you into growth.

If passion does not drive you, you will not grow. If you do not have a positive vision for your life, you will never move beyond where you are now. Find God's purpose. Seek it with your whole heart, then pursue it with your full passion. Keep that vision in mind. That will be the internal compass that keeps you on course.

THE BRUTAL FACTS

You cannot move forward until you face the truth about where you are.

To begin making progress toward your vision, you must begin with an honest assessment of who you are and where you are. Intentionally pursuing God's vision for your life is not the same as wishing for a happy ending, and it isn't a matter of glossing over the facts of your situation. You won't get from where you are now to your full potential without a heavy dose of self-examination. Surprisingly, the more honest you are about how bad your situation may be, the more likely you are to actually reach your full potential. Author Jim Collins refers to this as *The Stockdale Paradox*.

Admiral Jim Stockdale was the highest-ranking United States military officer held in the infamous "Hanoi Hilton" prisoner-of-war camp during the Vietnam War. Stockdale was imprisoned from 1965 to 1973 and was tortured more than twenty times. As a POW, Stockdale had no rights, no set release date, and no objective reason to believe he would see his home and family again. Despite this, he organized resistance against his captors and survived the brutal captivity for eight years. After his release, Stockdale was awarded the Congressional Medal of Honor.

When Jim Collins read *Love and War*, the book Stockdale coauthored with his wife, Collins couldn't imagine how anyone could survive that long and grueling ordeal—especially when he did not know what would happen, or whether he would ever see home again. How could anyone endure that without losing hope? "I never lost faith in the end of the story," Stockdale told Collins in an interview. "I never doubted not only that I would get out, but also that I would prevail in the end and turn the experience into the defining event of my life, which, in retrospect, I would not trade." Collins finishes the story this way:

> *I didn't say anything for many minutes, and we continued the slow walk toward the faculty club, Stockdale limping and arc-swinging his stiff leg that had never fully recovered from repeated torture. Finally, after about a hundred meters of silence, I asked, "Who didn't make it out?"*
>
> *"Oh, that's easy," he said. "The optimists."*
>
> *"The optimists? I don't understand," I said, now completely confused, given what he'd said a hundred meters earlier.*
>
> *"The optimists. Oh, they were the ones who said, 'We're going to be out by Christmas.' And Christmas would come, and Christmas would go. Then they'd say, 'We're going to be out by Easter.' And Easter would come, and Easter would go. And then Thanksgiving, and then it would be Christmas again. And they died of a broken heart."*
>
> *Another long pause, and more walking. Then he turned to me and said, "This is a very important lesson. You must never confuse faith that you will prevail in the end—which you can never afford to lose—with the discipline to confront the most brutal facts of your current reality, whatever they might be."*[2]

To reach your full potential, you must hold on to the positive vision you have for your life. Never lose that passion; never lose sight of that dream. However, you must also confront "the most brutal facts of your current reality, whatever they might be."

That phrase, *confront the brutal facts*, has become a buzzword in the business community, but it is really an old-fashioned concept. The Bible calls it *confession*. The apostle James writes, "Therefore confess your sins to one another and pray for each another so that you may be healed" (5:16 NIV), and the Proverbs tell us, "Whoever conceals their sins does not prosper, but the one who confesses and renounces them finds mercy" (28:13 NIV). The Bible puts it plainly: you cannot hope to move forward without coming to grips with your sins, failures, and shortcomings. You must admit to God, yourself, and possibly to others the reality of your situation, difficult though that may be.

Have you made a thorough assessment of your current reality? Are there hidden sins that need to be exposed to the light? Is there anything that you have been hiding from others, even from yourself, which you must confess to God? Allow the Holy Spirit to search your heart and shine light into your soul. Run to your Savior, the Lord Jesus Christ for forgiveness. Accept the divine witness that you are a child of God. This is the starting point for reaching your full potential.

You must assess your current reality in a temporal sense as well. What is the state of your education? Your health? Your marriage and family? Your finances? Your career? Where do you most need to grow? What are the obstacles that are now preventing you from growing? To whom do you need to make amends before you can move forward? Is there any need for restitution in your life? Make an exhaustive accounting of your mind, heart, body, finances, and relationships. You cannot reach your full potential until you know what is lacking in your current situation.

At the end of his life, the patriarch Jacob prophesied the future for each of his sons. He said of Joseph and his descendants, "Joseph is a fruitful vine, a fruitful vine near a spring, whose branches climb over a wall" (Genesis 49:22 NIV). The aged father knew that life would not always be easy for his descendants, but he believed they could "climb over" any obstacle. As you assess your current situation, it may seem that some of the obstacles you face are too great to overcome. They are not. Face the brutal facts of your situation, whatever they may be, but do not lose ultimate hope. Remember the vision to which God has called you. Imagine your life as it will be when you have reached your full potential. Let that vision sustain you.

THE INTERNAL ENGINE

Your motivation must come from within.

The First Industrial Revolution, which took place from around 1760 to 1840, dramatically changed life in the Western world. During this period, manual production of many goods, especially textiles, was replaced with mechanical production processes. Manufacturers created large factories, which employed many people, and there was a mass migration from the farm life of the countryside to the new, industrial cities. All of this was powered by steam engines. Steam engines use external combustion, meaning that the fuel is burned outside the engine itself, applying heat to the dynamic fluid, contained within the engine, through a wall or heat exchanger. Travelling by steam trains was effective over longer distances, but short-distance transportation was limited to horse and carriage. So the cities continued to grow.

Then in 1860, Belgian engineer J. Lenoi created the first internal combustion engine. Unlike steam engines, these new motors burned their fuel inside the engine, applying power directly to the piston. Internal combustion engines were lighter and more efficient than their counterparts. Within five years Karl Benz had built the first motor-driven vehicle. Known as "horseless carriages," these new vehicles began to replace the horse and buggy as a mode of personal transportation. By 1908, the Ford Motor Company was mass-producing cars, rolling 18,000 Model Ts off the assembly line that year. Car ownership spread rapidly, allowing greater individual freedom through personal transportation. Families that once flocked to the city for employment now drove to the outskirts of town for more personal space. The suburbs were born. In 2008 there were more than 248 million motor vehicles registered in the United States, about one for every 1.2 people.[3] Can anyone imagine life in our society without the automobile? And all of that was made possible by the simple switch from external to internal combustion. When you have a portable source of power, you have great freedom.

The lesson for reaching your full potential is that you too need internal, not external, power. Many people fail to reach their full potential because they are waiting for someone to come along and give them the motivation they need to get started. They are looking for a coach or cheerleader or leader to move them to their full potential. That will not happen, at least not for long. You must accept responsibility for motivating yourself and seeking the motivation that comes through the Spirit. You cannot wait for the right time, because there is never a right time. You can't wait for the right feeling, because you must learn to take action even when you don't feel like it. You will discover that being proactive will actually change the way you feel. No one else can change your destiny, either by getting you where God wants you to be or keeping you from getting there. You must have your own internal engine that keeps you moving forward. All change begins within; it is never external.

Those who continually require external motivation will never reach their full potential. If you constantly need others to affirm you, tell you what to do, or if you live your life to please them, you will not grow in the Spirit and achieve what God has for you. You must begin with a passion to achieve his purpose or calling for you. This will be the vision that empowers you, strengthens you during difficult times, and keeps you moving forward toward your full potential. Those who have a strong sense of purpose are more than spectators in life; they are active participants. They do not wait for change to happen; they bring change in their lives and in their community. If you are self-motivated, you will add value to others. Your soul winning will inspire others to win souls. Your worship will inspire others to worship. Your growth will inspire others to grow. That all begins with a passion to realize God's vision for your life.

The writer of Proverbs says, "Go to the ant, thou sluggard; consider her ways, and be wise: Which having no guide, overseer, or ruler, Provideth her meat in the summer, and gathereth her food in the harvest" (Prov. 6:6–8). These amazing little creatures need no one to tell them what to do. They see the need, and they take action. And as most of us know, it is nearly impossible to keep those tiny creatures from reaching their goal. Discover the power of internal motivation. Keep in touch with the Spirit, and do not look to others to move you forward. You know that you need to be active, to be purposeful, to take action in order to grow.

So do it!

GROWTH ACTIVITIES

All growth is intentional. You will not make progress in life by accident. This is something you must both choose to do and continually pursue. We also know that time is not an agent of change. While growth takes time, time alone does not produce the results you are after. You must be active in seeking growth. And you must have a compelling vision. Pain is a short-term motivator; passion will fuel you for the long run. Seek God's vision for your life and allow that to guide you forward. Do not gloss over the reality of your current situation. You must face the brutal facts in order to grow beyond them. Confess your sin where needed. Make restitution if called for. Look your situation squarely in the face without losing sight of God's vision for yourself. And then take action. You must motivate yourself for this journey. No one can do this for you. It is up to you to seek the Spirit, keep a positive attitude, and keep growing.

To discover your purpose and move toward your full potential, you need practical steps. You won't reach your potential in a single day or even one year, but you can take the first steps on that journey today. Here are some practical things you can do right now to put purpose to work in your life.

WAIT ON THE WORD

At this point in the change process, you may become impatient for results or frustrated at your lack of progress—even ashamed of some early failures. Don't allow mistakes to stop you; growing on purpose is a continual work that you will never want to stop, especially when you begin to see results.

Don't allow a lack of understanding to keep you from the positive changes that are required for spiritual advancement.

Think about the experience of Joseph, whom we talked about earlier. The Psalm writer says this about Joseph's experience in prison: "He sent a man before them, even Joseph, who was sold for a servant: Whose feet they hurt with fetters: he was laid in iron: Until the time that his word came: the word of the LORD tried him. The king sent and loosed him; even the ruler of the people, and let him go free" (Ps. 105:17–20). The king did not set Joseph free until the Word had tried him. He had to grow to be free. You cannot progress further if you don't acquire knowledge you need to grow. So seek the Lord through his Word, and wait on the Word patiently.

The hardest part in receiving any prophetic word is waiting until it comes to pass. As it was with Joseph so shall it be with you. Don't expect to get there in one quick leap. Pace yourself and don't give up!

CONDUCT A SELF-INVENTORY

Make a fearless personal inventory of your heart, your mind, your relationships, and every aspect of your life. Every leader needs to have a heart-to-heart talk with himself or herself and prayerfully consider these questions. Write down your answers so you can refer to them and be guided by them.

Are there unconfessed sins in my life? If so, what will I do about them?

Are my relationships with my family members, friends, and fellow church members in order?

- What is the state of my personal finances?
- What are the top five areas in which I need to grow?
- Do I have a personal growth plan?

- How consistently do I practice the Rule of Five?
- How consistently do I practice other spiritual disciplines?
- Am I helping others grow to their full potential?

If you are going to grow, you must grow on purpose. Intentional, purposeful, and planned growth is the only way to cultivate your attitude and character. In turn, when you grow it will build influence because you will grow virtues that will impact and affect the people around you.

ASSEMBLE RESOURCES

A resource is anything that helps you achieve a goal, and that resource does not have to be tangible. Think broadly about the things that will help you grow on purpose, and begin to assemble. Here are some suggested resources. You may add others of your own.

- Your Rule of Five
- A Bible
- A Daily Prayer Time
- A Place to Serve Others
- Spiritually Enriching Books
- A Regimen of Physical Exercise
- An Accountability Partner
- Create a Change Team

You will gain the most from this process if you have a team of others who help you, hold you accountable, and whom you also help to reach their full potential. Assemble a Change Team of three to six other persons with whom you can share what you are learning. Ideally, you would meet together each week to discuss what you are reading in this book, share your experiences, and encourage one another to keep growing. If you cannot meet together, create a virtual Change Team via video chat, social media, or email. Enlist others to help you along the way.

KEEP A CHANGE LOG

You are learning a great deal already in this process, but you will likely forget it quickly if you do not make notes. Begin keeping a Change Log, or journal, of your thoughts, learnings, experiences, goals, and prayers. Remember that this Change Log is for you alone. What you write there will stay between you and God unless you choose to share it, so write freely. You will find that the discipline of writing will help clarify your thinking as well as reinforce your memory. This will become a time when the Spirit can speak to you.

In your Change Log, pay close attention to any negative thoughts or emotions. Writing about them will expose them to light and help you avoid being trapped by them. Remember that you are a child of the King. Write positive affirmations and record the promises of God. This will strengthen and encourage you.

I really believe you can do this. I know that you may have tried and failed in the past to be fully faithful at pursuing God's best for yourself. Put those thoughts aside. That is the past; you are now focused on a beautiful new future. Envision what your life will look like in one year from now, five years, and ten years. Keep that vision before you. Make the most of every day, and do not become discouraged. You are on the road to a bright future!

ACTION LIST

1. Pray and search the Word to discover your purpose (be patient).
2. Conduct a self-inventory.
3. List the top five areas in which you need to grow.
4. Assemble the resources you need in order to grow.
5. Enlist a Change Team.
6. Begin a Change Log.
7. Share Strategy No. 1: Discover Your Purpose with one person today.

STRATEGY NO. 2

Accept Personal Responsibility

You Are Responsible for Your Own Growth

> *Work out your own salvation with fear and trembling. For it is God which worketh in you both to will and to do of his good pleasure.*
> *—Philippians 2:12–13*

If you have had the privilege of raising children, as I have, then you know something about the need for accepting personal responsibility. Teaching children to be responsible for themselves is a major part of any parent's job, and it is challenging. There is something in each of us that makes us crave freedom without responsibility. Occasionally that produces a humorous result, as in the case of one father and son that I heard about. The teenage boy had taken an interest in body building, and his dad, though skeptical, accompanied him to a sporting goods store to look at weight-lifting equipment. The son zeroed in on a particular weight set and pleaded with his father to purchase it. "Please, Dad," he begged, "I promise I'll use it every day."

"I don't know," the father replied, "It's really a commitment on your part."

"Please, Dad," the young teen insisted.

"They're not cheap," the father said.

"I'll use them, Dad, I promise. You'll see."

Probably every parent has had some such conversation about sporting equipment, a musical instrument, or a pet. Countless moms and dads have done just as this father did. Believing that his young son could live up to the responsibility of ownership, the dad went to the counter and paid for the weights, then headed for the door. He had taken only a few steps when he heard his son call out, "You mean I have to carry them to the car?"

Like that teenage boy, many of us set out on the journey to reach our full potential but have no idea how much effort it will require. Having determined to make a change in our lives, we are convinced it will come quickly and easily, and often make grandiose statements about our future performance. Like Peter, who made exaggerated claims of loyalty to Jesus at the Last Supper, we cannot know how much will soon be required of us. We believe we know what it will take to reach our potential, but we cannot know for sure until we begin.

Change always takes longer and requires more effort than we think. Though the Holy Ghost is capable of transforming your life in an instant, God rarely chooses to work that way. Growing to your full potential will likely take some time and will require sustained effort on your part. You must take responsibility for that process, choosing daily to cooperate with the Spirit in your complete transformation.

While some who seek growth are simply naïve about the responsibility involved, others are fully aware of the discipline that will be required but try to avoid it. They want the result without the effort. They are a bit like the nurse's aide and housekeeper who got into a dispute about cleaning up a spill on the hospital floor. A patient had spilled a cup of water, and, concerned that he might slip and fall, called a nurse's aide for help. Little did he realize that the hospital had an unusual policy about spills. If the spill was small, the nursing staff was required to clean it up. However, larger spills were the responsibility of the housekeeping department. The aide looked at the spill and judged it to be a large one, so she called housekeeping. The housekeeper, however, took a different view. An argument ensured.

"It's a large puddle," the aide said, "It's not my job."

"Well it's not mine either," the housekeeper shot back. "That puddle is too small."

This went on for some time. Finally, the frustrated patient took the water pitcher from his nightstand and dumped it on the floor. "Is that big enough?" he asked, putting an end to the argument.

Some who seek to reach their full potential are a bit like those underachieving employees: they believe someone else should be responsible for their growth. "God knows where I am," they say. "If he wants to change me, I'm ready." Or they may think change depends on someone else's action. "If my spouse would help out, then I could change," some say. Or, "There's no way I can grow while I'm stuck in this job (or church, or house, or family)."

This is where Strategy No. 2 comes in: *Accept Personal Responsibility*. If you are to grow to your potential in Christ, you must learn to apply this simple truth to your life: You are responsible for your own growth. No one else can do this for you. Even God will not change your life without your cooperation.

You must take ownership of your life and your future.

Scripture teaches this principle time and time again, perhaps most clearly in Paul's letter to the Galatian church. The apostle writes:

> *For every man shall bear his own burden. Let him that is taught in the word communicate unto him that teacheth in all good things. Be not deceived; God is not mocked: for whatsoever a man soweth, that shall he also reap. For he that soweth to his flesh shall of the flesh reap corruption; but he that soweth to the Spirit shall of the Spirit reap life everlasting. And let us not be weary in well doing: for in due season we shall reap, if we faint not. (Gal. 6:5–9)*

You are responsible for your life and for the choices that will lead you either to growth or stagnation. It is easy to fall into a victim mentality, believing that others have made the choices that will determine your future. Nothing could be further from the truth. You have the power and responsibility to choose your attitude and your actions. Though you cannot control what happens to you, you can control how you respond to it. You can control what you become. To reach your full potential, you must take responsibility.

Let's explore this strategy by examining four key concepts. They are:

- Self-Leadership
- Self-Motivation
- Self-Discipline
- Self-Multiplication

These concepts flesh out the strategy of accepting personal responsibility. By understanding and applying them to your life, you will move from a victim mind-set to that of a leader. Then we will explore the practical steps that will help you cultivate a closer relationship with your heavenly Father so that you can grow into that responsibility. At the conclusion of this chapter, you will understand the critical importance of taking responsibility for your choices, you will be motivated to put that knowledge into practice, and you will have a realistic action plan for taking ownership of your most important resource—yourself.

SELF-LEADERSHIP

You set the direction for your own life.

Think about this for a moment. Who is the person that you spend the most time with? Who has the most power in your life? Who is the person with the greatest ability to help you grow? Who has most often foiled your plans to do the right thing? Whom do you know better than anyone else? The obvious answer is you. That is why learning to lead yourself is one of the most important things you will ever do. If you hope to reach your full potential or to lead others, you must first be an effective leader of yourself. A Chinese maxim says, "He who can govern himself is fit to govern the world." Your journey to full potential in Christ begins right here in your own heart and mind.

MASTER YOUR MIND

The first step in self-leadership is to master your own thoughts. The apostle Paul gave us great advice on reaching our full potential in Christ when he wrote, "And be not conformed to this world:

but be ye transformed by the renewing of your mind, that ye may prove what is that good, and acceptable, and perfect, will of God" (Rom. 12:2). Notice the progression in this simple verse. First, we refuse to accept the values, opinions, and judgments of the world. We do not conform to this world or its culture. So much about the way the world thinks is exactly contrary to the life in Christ that you are pursuing. Do not blindly accept the financial values, standards of beauty, life goals, or moral standards of those around you. Think for yourself. Begin to understand the ways of Christ. Dwell on them. Own them. Where do you let your thoughts dwell when you are bored or alone? What are you doing to fill your mind with wholesome, positive thinking? Are you aware of the ways in which your thinking may really be more like the world than like the Word of God? Self-leadership begins with gaining control of your mind.

Next, we see that this refusal to conform to the negative and destructive ways of the world produces a renewed mind. Before long, you will have a completely different way of thinking. You will value humility over pride, people over things, and justice over wealth. As Jesus taught us, your actions spring from your inner thoughts and attitudes: "A good man out of the good treasure of his heart bringeth forth that which is good; and an evil man out of the evil treasure of his heart bringeth forth that which is evil: for of the abundance of the heart his mouth speaketh" (Luke 6:45).

Finally, we are fully transformed. How? By the renewing of the mind. When you gain control of your thoughts and attitudes, you gain control of yourself. You begin to allow the Holy Ghost to pour into you the wholesome, hopeful, positive thoughts and attitudes that will lead you to reach your full potential. Before long, you will see that transformation take place in your actions and interactions with others. You will become a different person.

ELIMINATE NEGATIVE SELF-TALK

Self-leadership begins with getting control of your mind, and that includes this important practice: eliminate negative self-talk. You have the power to either build yourself up or tear yourself down. Too often we make terrible judgments about ourselves without realizing what we are doing. Have you ever said, "How could I be so stupid?" or "What an idiot! I can't believe I did that." How about this one: "I guess I can't do anything right." Get control of those thoughts right away. Banish them from your thinking. Refuse to allow them space in your heart. Remember the words of scripture: "The Spirit itself beareth witness with our spirit, that we are the children of God" (Rom. 8:16). Accept God's judgment about yourself. You are his precious child.

CHOOSE GOOD COMPANIONS

Self-leadership also means choosing companions wisely. I have found that there are certain types of people that it is best to avoid, or at least limit my exposure to. Among them are perpetual victims. These are the folk who always think their problems are someone else's fault. They refuse to accept responsibility and are always looking for someone to join them in self-pity. I also limit my time around complainers. These are the folk who see only problems, never solutions. They would rather do nothing and feel bad about life than take positive steps to improve their situation. I also avoid carnally minded people, those who are constantly pursuing the things of the flesh rather than the things of the Spirit. Please note that I do not avoid spending time with those who need salvation. Although I don't buy into their way of thinking, I love them and seek to share good news with them. Rather, I'm talking about believers who are more focused on the things of this world than on pleasing God. I can't afford to let their materialism or lustfulness or selfishness infect my heart.

Does this sound harsh? Remember the words of David: "Blessed is the man that walketh not in the counsel of the ungodly, nor standeth in the way of sinners, nor sitteth in the seat of the scornful. But his delight is in the law of the Lord; and in his law doth he meditate day and night" (Ps. 1:1–2). Your companions have great influence over you; choose them wisely. It has been said that you are the sum of the five people you spend the most time with. If that is true, what would the aggregate of your five closest friends look like? Would that resemble a godly person who is pursuing God's full potential for his or her life? Would it be a complainer? A gossip? Are you spending time with those who are, like you, bent on achieving their full potential? If not, how do those relationships affect your outlook and your actions? Seek companions who are likeminded and will support you in your desire to grow. You need kindred spirits to help you on your journey.

FLEE FROM SELF-PITY

Finally, self-leadership means avoiding self-pity. Everyone feels this at some point, but some people seem to have a penchant for feeling sorry for themselves. After being disappointed by a friend, rejected by a spouse, or failing to reach an important goal, it is natural to feel sad. However, beware of allowing that feeling to dwell in your heart. It has the potential to derail your journey to reach your full potential. Self-pity is paralyzing. It can become a blanket in which you wrap yourself to protect you from further hurt. That feels good for a moment, but it can become a trap that lasts a lifetime. You will never move forward in life while you spend time dwelling on the hurts and disappointments of the past. Banish self-pity by giving praise to God. Paul wrote, "In every thing give thanks: for this is the will of God in Christ Jesus concerning you" (1 Thess. 5:18). Take control of your mind and heart, and refuse to allow a victim mentality to root you in place.

SELF-MOTIVATION

Only you can inspire yourself to grow.

The second concept you'll need to understand to implement the strategy of personal responsibility is self-motivation. We have talked about self-motivation already in the previous chapter. However, this subject is so vital for your success that it warrants a second look. To take responsibility for your growth, you must learn to motivate yourself. If you depend on others to inspire or push you toward reaching your potential, you will almost certainly fail. The best motivation always comes from within.

When England's Queen Victoria was a child, she was unaware that she would be the future monarch. As a result, she frustrated her tutors by her lackadaisical attitude and sometimes-rebellious behavior. They simply couldn't motivate her. They had tried everything to get her to behave properly and to study, but nothing worked. Finally, her teachers decided to tell her the whole truth: she would someday rule the British Empire. Upon hearing that, the young Victoria said simply, "Then I will be good." The realization that she was a royal person with a high calling gave the princess a newfound sense of responsibility. It motivated her behavior from that day forward.

To reach your potential, you must find that same kind of inner motivation. No one else can persuade you to make the sacrifices, spend the time, and acquire the discipline you will need to grow to maturity in Christ. Your parents cannot do it. Your friends cannot. Not even your pastor can give you that motivation. It must come from within.

People who rely on other sources to move them into action are usually interested in doing the minimum required to get by. They do what they have to, nothing more. Truly inspired people are self-motivated. They want to add value to others and make a difference. So where does this self-motivation come from? Here are three sources of positive energy you can tap into.

YOUR VISION

The word *vision* simply means a divine perspective on your purpose. When you can picture God's future, it will energize you to achieve your best. Once you have a clear picture of your purpose it will raise the level of your motivation, and you will be ready to lead others into their purpose. If you have not yet discovered your purpose, keep praying and seeking. When you have discovered your purpose, keep that vision before you constantly. Say it to yourself every day. Write it in places where you will see it often. Make your vision come alive by writing it as if it were reality. Let that vision motivate you to keep going.

YOUR HABITS

Your vision will not be achieved in one grand sweep. There is no single dramatic action that will catapult you to being holier, more effective in ministry, or a better spouse or parent. Instead, you reach your goal through a long series of smaller actions that become habits in your life. There is no pill that will make you more disciplined. However, as you read Scripture and pray each day, day in and day out, even when you don't feel like it, you become a disciplined person. Goals without habits are like a car with no tires. The engine may fire; but unless the rubber meets the road, the vehicle cannot move forward.

Build good habits into your life, and eliminate bad ones. By taking even small actions toward your goal, you will multiply your motivation. You will find that motivation builds on itself, so these actions become something you desire. What kind of habits do we mean? Get proper sleep. Spend time with God every day. Practice your Rule of Five. Exercise. These seemingly trivial things will make you healthier and stronger. They will build your motivation to do the harder work of making substantive changes in your life.

It is an unfortunate fact of life that people who are not self-motivated do everything they can to keep those who are self-motivated from living out God's vision for their lives. When you allow the thoughts, attitudes, and expectations of others to seep into your thinking, it will sap your motivation. When you adopt positive associations and practices, you will strengthen your motivation. Eliminate negative friendships and behaviors and replace them with positive ones. Take the right steps, do the right things, and your motivation will follow.

YOUR STRATEGY

Without a strategic plan of action, you will burn up energy that can't be replaced by any external force. Set your path and establish your direction. Then create a plan for growth and move toward that goal regardless of how you feel at any given moment. Make your vision concrete by adding specific action steps to move forward. A goal with no strategy can seem overwhelming. A strategic plan with small, doable actions is motivating. And as you begin this walk, you will receive the positive energy and motivation that comes only from taking right actions.

Always make your strategic steps *S.M.A.R.T.* That is, make your plans *specific, measurable, actionable, realistic,* and *time-bound.* State exactly what you will do, be sure that it can be objectively measured, begin your statement with a verb, check to see that it is achievable, and set a deadline. Here is an example of a *S.M.A.R.T.* objective:

- Poor: Spend more time with God.
- Better: Read Scripture and pray for fifteen minutes each day at 7:00 a.m.
- Poor: Become the best spouse ever.
- Better: Set an appointment with my pastor for marital counseling within the next two weeks.

Having a clear strategic plan will motivate you to take action. What is the first problem you need to solve in order to reach your goal? What is the next step to take in pursuing your vision? What strategic actions will move you forward? Write down your plan, then do it. This is scriptural. "And the Lord answered me, and said, Write the vision, and make it plain upon tables, that he may run that readeth it" (Hab. 2:2).

When you depend entirely on external factors to create your motivation, you doom yourself to a life of unfulfilled potential. When you take responsibility for setting your direction and motivating yourself to move toward it, you will achieve your potential. Only you can lead yourself forward.

SELF-DISCIPLINE

Only you can do your work.

A third aspect of personal responsibility is self-discipline. Responsibility is a personal ability and accountability to take action without the authority of someone else. If you are responsible for your own growth, then only you can do the work that is required to achieve it. To implement the strategy of accepting personal responsibility in your life, you must discipline yourself to faithfully do all the things you must do and to avoid doing the things you should not. Responsibility depends on self-discipline.

The writer of Proverbs says, "He that hath no rule over his own spirit is like a city that is broken down, and without walls" (25:28). A city without walls is open and undefended, vulnerable to an attack by the enemy. You cannot overcome attacks from your enemy, the devil, if you do not first build some walls around your mind, your heart, and your actions. That's where self-discipline comes in. It is the ability to guard yourself and your actions to avoid being pulled away from God's design for your life. You must control your own appetites and desires or the enemy will use them against you.

TAKE SMALL ACTIONS

Self-discipline sounds ominous, but it is a tremendously positive thing. Taking small, simple, daily actions builds tremendous power over time. The Proverbs teach us that "the sluggard will not plow by reason of the cold; therefore shall he beg in harvest, and have nothing" (20:4). However, "he who gathers crops in summer is a prudent son" (Prov. 10:5 NIV). When you harness the power of daily habits—that is, doing the right thing, even in small ways, on a daily basis—you build discipline into your life. This is why the Rule of Five is so important to your spiritual growth. By practicing that habit, you build good things into your life—*and* you strengthen your ability to act in positive ways. That's self-discipline! What habits do you need to drop in order to become more disciplined? What habits would you like to acquire to make yourself more likely to reach your full potential? When will you start?

MAKE NO EXCUSES

To acquire self-discipline, you must resolve to be done with excuse making. Again, the writer of Proverbs brings a great insight, saying, "The slothful man saith, There is a lion without, I shall be slain in the streets" (22:13). People who lack self-discipline always have a reason why today is not the right day to take action. It's too hot. It's too cold. It would be better to start on a Monday. I'm too tired. I just need a little more time. Tomorrow I will. Excuse making is the enemy of responsibility. Discipline yourself to take action by refusing to make excuses, defer, or delay. Do it now.

When you are tempted to believe you don't have the time, energy, or resources to take action, think about Nehemiah. He faced great opposition in rebuilding the broken-down walls of Jerusalem. He had both political enemies and hostile forces against him. Yet he refused to put off this important task. Rather than take a break from rebuilding in order to fight other battles, Nehemiah outfitted each builder with a weapon, and they continued to work. "They which builded on the wall, and they that bare burdens, with those that laded, every one with one of his hands wrought in the work, and with the other hand held a weapon. For the builders, every one had his sword girded by his side, and so builded. And he that sounded the trumpet was by me" (Neh. 4:17–18). Don't tolerate excuse making in yourself. Certainly you will face obstacles on your journey to full potential. Never allow them to derail you. Do what it takes to be successful.

DON'T STOP

Acquiring self-discipline depends on building momentum. Have you ever noticed that you want to do more of what you are currently doing? When you are cleaning the house, it's easier to tackle one more room when you see the results of the first effort. When you go for a run or a bike ride, the hardest part is getting started. Once you get out and get going you want to continue, but stop for too long and it's hard to start again. Our actions build momentum, either positive or negative. That's why it's crucial to keep practicing your positive habits and disciplines even when you don't feel like it. One break in the chain can derail you, and then it will be more difficult to re-establish your self-discipline. Read Scripture even when you are busy. Go to church even when you've been out late the previous night. Keep doing small, positive, daily actions no matter how you feel. Your self-discipline will build upon itself.

SELF-MULTIPLICATION

When you teach others, you grow faster.

The fourth element of personal responsibility is self-multiplication. One of the internal battles you will face as you grow is a secret desire to keep what you are learning to yourself. Hoarding information, ideas, and experiences is a natural tendency, and a selfish one. Somehow we fear that by giving away hard-won knowledge or opportunities we place ourselves at a disadvantage. In fact the opposite is true. You grow faster and better when you teach others. You gain even more when you give what you have away.

Jesus put it this way, "Give, and it shall be given unto you; good measure, pressed down, and shaken together, and running over, shall men give into your bosom. For with the same measure that ye mete withal it shall be measured to you again" (Luke 6:38). The immediate context of this verse is money; Jesus is talking about being generous financially or materially. Yet this concept applies to much more than finances. When you are generous with knowledge, ideas, and experiences, you gain more as well. Paul writes, "But this I say, He which soweth sparingly shall reap also sparingly; and he which soweth bountifully shall reap also bountifully" (2 Cor. 9:6). When you give, you gain.

Teaching others what you are learning will both multiply your effectiveness as a leader and accelerate your own growth. When you say what you have discovered aloud to someone else, you internalize the truth and own it in a deeper way. When you show a friend how to do something, you learn the process even better. When you share an experience with another person, it becomes more powerful in your mind and memory. When you give away an idea, you are sure to discover ten more.

Jesus' strategy for building the church was not addition but multiplication. Reproduce yourself by mentoring others. Lead others to Christ, teaching them what you are learning. Lead others on the journey of reaching your potential. Whom can you bring along with you as you grow spiritually? How can you share these ideas with others? Do that, and you will both gain.

GROWTH ACTIVITIES

Now that you have a handle on the meaning of accepting personal responsibility, it's time to put that into action with some practical action steps. The apostle Peter wrote, "Wherefore the rather, brethren, give diligence to make your calling and election sure: for if ye do these things, ye shall never fall" (2 Pet. 1:10). You are responsible to take action on what you have learned and to follow the vision God has placed within your heart. We are all responsible for our own growth. Remember, the purpose of this book is to help you grow to your full potential by having a deep, personal relationship with God. It would be a mistake to think of spiritual activities as somehow different from the practical strategies we have been learning. Spiritual actions are highly practical. The following practical steps are exactly what you need to take responsibility for your life and grow to your full potential. If you have been a Christian for a while, these steps may seem obvious and elementary, but let me assure you they are not. Being proactive in reaching your full potential begins with establishing the spiritual disciplines that will further your relationship with the Lord. You need the disciplines of *prayer, Scripture, fasting, worship,* and *witness.*

DEVELOP A DAILY HABIT OF PRAYER

You have a responsibility to pray. Having others pray for you is great, but you must have your own faithful prayer life in order to develop a relationship with God. There are times in life where you have to submit to a word from the Lord regarding decisions in your life. That makes it vital to know his voice. You develop that familiarity through consistent, daily prayer. And this practice of prayer must be a habit, not a last resort. If you only pray when you're in trouble, you're in trouble. Develop a daily habit of personal prayer. Jesus said, "But thou, when thou prayest, enter into thy closet, and when thou hast shut thy door, pray to thy Father which is in secret; and thy Father which seeth in secret shall reward thee openly" (Matt. 6:6). When you are faithful to pray, God is faithful to answer. What is your current practice of prayer? If it is not a consistent daily pattern, what will you do to establish that habit?

READ AND STUDY SCRIPTURE CONSISTENTLY

You have a responsibility to know Scripture. There is no substitute for knowledge of God's Word. It is one of the things that will fuel your growth in the Spirit. Paul wrote, "Study to shew thyself approved unto God, a workman that needeth not to be ashamed, rightly dividing the word of truth" (2 Tim. 2:15). And John reminds us, "In the beginning was the Word, and the Word was with God, and the Word was God" (John 1:1). If you want to know God, then you must know his Word.

This includes both reading and study of the Bible. There is a difference between the two. Bible reading is a personal spiritual discipline, something you do on your own as a means of seeking God. It involves reading and reflecting on his Word. As you read, the Holy Spirit will open your mind to Scripture. You will come to love and understand God by reading devotionally.

Bible study is a more formal discipline that is often (though not always) practiced in a group. When you investigate the Bible by delving deeper into a passage, learning about the historical context, studying the meaning of various words, and seeing how it relates to other parts of the Bible, you will grow intellectually as well as spiritually. Both reading and study are important disciplines. What is your current practice of Scripture reading and study? How might you further your spiritual growth by strengthening this vital discipline?

FAST REGULARLY

You have a responsibility to fast. Fasting is vital to our walk with God. The Lord spoke through the prophet Isaiah, saying, "Is not this the fast that I have chosen? to loose the bands of wickedness, to undo the heavy burdens, and to let the oppressed go free, and that ye break every yoke?" (Isa. 58:6). In the Gospel of Matthew, Jesus said, "when ye fast" (Matt. 6:16), not *if* you fast. This lets us know that fasting is not optional. Elsewhere, Jesus taught that some things are achieved only through prayer and fasting (see Mark 9:29).

Fasting may be the most neglected of all spiritual practices in our day. Yet when you pray and fast, the Holy Ghost is able to work in your heart in ways that would not otherwise be possible. When you experience hunger, your mind is directed back to God and to his Word. You will begin to see the ways that you depend on other things, including food, for comfort and strength, rather than relying on God. When you fast, you grow. There is great power in fasting.

When was the last time you fasted? What were the results of that fast? How will you deepen your relationship with God through the practice of fasting?

WORSHIP WITH YOUR CHURCH CONSISTENTLY

You have a responsibility to gather with the body. Christians should regard it as a sacred duty to meet together for the worship of God. Isolation or separation brings devastation. No one is an island, as the poet John Donne put it. We all need each other. The writer of Hebrews made that clear when he wrote, "Not forsaking the assembling of ourselves together, as the manner of some is; but exhorting one another: and so much the more, as ye see the day approaching" (10:25). We need one another for strength, encouragement, and accountability.

You receive things from God in church that you can't receive anywhere else. Your private prayer closet is important, but that is not the same as corporate worship. Your time in prayer will empower you so when you come into the assembly you are able to impact others. You must be in close proximity with others in order to impact them. You must gather together. And when you come to church, enter into the service with an attitude of worship. Do not expect to be amused or entertained. Reverently seek whatever God will do or say in that worship experience.

How consistently do you gather with your church for worship? How do you prepare yourself to enter into that experience? What will you do to strengthen your relationship with God through worship?

WITNESS FOR JESUS AT EVERY OPPORTUNITY

You have a responsibility to share the good news about Jesus with others. The Great Commission still stands as the main objective and mission statement of the church. To accomplish that mission, God always uses people's voices. Everything in the kingdom is "voice activated." God spoke the world into existence. Salvation comes by use of the voice. The name of Jesus is spoken over us at baptism, and the Holy Ghost is a voice as our guide and comforter. Jesus said, "Go ye into all the world, and preach the gospel to every creature" (Mark 16:15), and he added, "But ye shall receive power, after that the Holy Ghost is come upon you: and ye shall be witnesses unto me both in Jerusalem, and in all Judaea, and in Samaria, and unto the uttermost part of the earth" (Acts 1:8).

When you speak the gospel to others, you fulfill your responsibility as a witness. You offer salvation to others, and strengthen your own faith through obedience. Do not pass up an opportunity to witness in the name of Jesus. You do not have to wait for the Holy Ghost to make you ready to witness—you are already commissioned to do it! Give God the glory when good things come into your life. Praise God through difficult times. Speak the name of Jesus to those who are lost and in need of hope. "Be ready always to give an answer to every man that asketh you a reason of the hope that is in you with meekness and fear" (1 Pet. 3:15).

How would you characterize your practice of witnessing? Is it active and growing? Sporadic? Non-existent? Do not allow fear to keep you from practicing a discipline that will cause you to grow spiritually by leaps and bounds. With whom could you share a simple testimony about Jesus today?

You are responsible for your own growth. You must be proactive, self-motivated, and disciplined if you are to grow to your full potential. You will make greater progress as you lead not only yourself but also others on this journey. Your principal tools for accepting personal responsibility are spiritual tools: prayer, Scripture, fasting, worship, and witness. Though this sounds daunting, there is no reason to fear. You have great potential, and I believe you will rise up and take responsibility for reaching it. Here's to your future in the Kingdom!

ACTION LIST

1. Make a list of the things (such as thoughts, actions, attitudes, or even people) that negatively affect your growth. State how you will reduce that negative effect.

2. If you have not yet identified your purpose, spend time in prayer seeking God's purpose for your life. If you have discovered your purpose, share it with one person.

3. List three positive habits that you will develop to further your growth. Be specific about when, where, and how you will practice them.

4. Assess your current practice of prayer, Scripture, fasting, worship, and witness. State what you will do to strengthen your discipline in each area.

5. Share Strategy No. 2: Accept Personal Responsibility with one person today.

STRATEGY NO. 3

Take Spiritual Authority

You Already Have What You Need to Reach Your Full Potential

And when he had called unto him his twelve disciples, he gave them power against unclean spirits, to cast them out, and to heal all manner of sickness and all manner of disease.
—Matthew 10:1

He was about twelve years old. That was too young to follow his brothers into the army, and too old to stay home and do nothing. Not that his job was unimportant. Somebody had to tend the farm and produce supplies for the army, fighting at the front. Yet this preteen, as we would call him now, longed for more. He had vision. He had skill. He had courage. He was determined to take part in the grand battle that everyone knew was coming, the decisive conflict that would determine the future of his nation. So when his father, Jesse, loaded him up with supplies and sent him off to the front lines to check on his brothers, David was only too ready to oblige.

Goliath of Gath, the champion of the Philistine army, was a literal giant, standing over nine feet tall and possessing amazing strength. The tip of his spear weighed the same as a bowling ball. Outfitted in full armor, he was a fearsome sight to behold. Each day Goliath stepped out from the Philistine camp and challenged the Israelites. "I defy the armies of Israel this day," he shouted. "Give me a man, that we may fight together" (1 Sam. 17:10). All the Israelite soldiers, including David's older brothers and even their king, cowered in fear. By the time boy David arrived, this standoff had been going on for over forty days.

David, with naïveté born of simple faith, demanded to know why no one was willing to go out and face the giant. His brothers scoffed at him; others ignored him. Finally, David took his offer to the king. "And David said to Saul, Let no man's heart fail because of him; thy servant will go and fight with this Philistine" (1 Sam. 17:32).

You may know how the story goes from here. If not, take a few moments to read about this epic combat in 1 Samuel 17. Armed only with a slingshot and five smooth stones, the intrepid boy went out to face the giant. Goliath was not amused. "Am I a dog, that thou comest to me with staves?" he asked. Raging, scoffing, cursing David by unholy gods, this hulk of a man sneered at the boy, "Come to me, and I will give thy flesh unto the fowls of the air, and to the beasts of the field" (1 Sam. 17:43–44). That prompted one of the most courageous speeches in all of Scripture. David answered:

> *Thou comest to me with a sword, and with a spear, and with a shield: but I come to thee in the name of the Lord of hosts, the God of the armies of Israel, whom thou hast defied.*

> *This day will the Lord deliver thee into mine hand; and I will smite thee, and take thine head from thee; and I will give the carcasses of the host of the Philistines this day unto the fowls of the air, and to the wild beasts of the earth; that all the earth may know that there is a God in Israel.*
>
> *And all this assembly shall know that the Lord saveth not with sword and spear: for the battle is the Lord's, and he will give you into our hands.* (1 Sam. 17:45–47)

With that, the two warriors charged at each other. David reached into his shepherd's bag and produced one stone. He placed it into his sling and whirled it around and around and around, then let it go. The stone hit Goliath smack in the forehead, driving deep into his skull. The massive giant stopped in his tracks, tottered in slow motion for a moment, then fell facedown with a resounding thud. David rushed to him, snatched the massive sword from Goliath's own hand, and with it hacked off the giant's head. The Philistine army fled in terror; the Israelites rallied and pursued, winning a great victory on that historic day.

The story of David and Goliath is well known even to those outside the community of faith. The very words *David and Goliath* have come to symbolize the classic underdog situation in which a smaller, more righteous hero defeats a larger, less honorable opponent. And therein lies the secret to David's victory and to your eventual success in reaching your full potential. For in God's economy, the race is not to the swift or the battle to the strong, but victory goes to those who trust in the Lord. That brings us to Strategy No. 3 for growing to your full potential: *Take Spiritual*

Authority. This strategy rests on a simple, biblical truth. Mark it well: You already have what you need to reach your full potential.

What gave David, who was younger, smaller, weaker, and less experienced than Goliath, the ability—to say nothing of the courage—to prevail? It was spiritual authority. David came to the battle armed not with superior weapons or strength but with the power that comes from being called by God, sent forth on God's business, and acting in simple faith. He had spiritual authority because he acted under God's divine authority. Spiritual authority is what enables an inarticulate fisherman like Simon Peter to preach eloquently on the day of Pentecost, ushering some three thousand souls into the Kingdom. Spiritual authority is what enabled a failed missionary by the name of John Wesley, after his heart was "strangely warmed" by the Holy Ghost, to ignite a revival movement that swept across two continents in the 1700s. Spiritual authority explains how "five of you shall chase an hundred, and an hundred of you shall put ten thousand to flight" (Lev. 26:8). And spiritual authority is what you need to overcome the "giants" in your life.

Think about the giants you face right now. I don't mean actual giants like Goliath but the huge obstacles that stand between you and reaching your full potential. You may be facing a mountain of debt. It calls out to you every time you get a bill in the mail, saying, "I defy you to go further in life! You are stuck right where you are!" Your giant might be a relationship with someone that is out of order in your life. It could be tension in your marriage, or even an illicit entanglement. The problem looms so large it overwhelms you. Perhaps you face the need to forgive someone who has harmed you, to break the chain of an addictive behavior, or to confront a person or situation that frightens you. These situations seem impossible. In your heart, you think, "The difficulties are so large and I am so small, I cannot possibly overcome them." You may identify with David's brothers, cowering in the face of a giant, not realizing that you have the greatest power in heaven or on earth available to you—the power of the Holy Ghost.

As a believer in Christ, you are already empowered by God to transform your life and reach your full potential. You have received the Holy Spirit. You have been commissioned as a soldier in Christ's army. You have been sent forth to be transformed and transform others. You have spiritual authority.

Too many people fail to reach their potential because they do not believe they can. They think their problems are insurmountable, or that they need something else—more training, more motivation, more resources, maybe even someone's permission—to move forward. Here is good news: You already have all of that. You have the Holy Ghost to guide and enable you, and you have God's commission to go forth and conquer. You already have the spiritual authority you need to move forward.

Let's examine spiritual authority in more detail so that you will understand how it functions and be able to apply it in your life. There are five levels of spiritual authority. They are:

- Calling
- Character
- Commitment
- Consistency
- Conviction

As we explore each level, you will come to see from where spiritual authority comes and why it is so important for your spiritual growth. You will see the areas in which you need to accept a greater level of spiritual authority. Finally, we will identify some practical activities that will help you grow in this area. When we are finished, you will have a clear plan of action for taking spiritual authority in your life.

LEVEL 1: CALLING

Spiritual authority is derived from God's call on your life.

The first level of spiritual authority is *calling*. Your spiritual authority is derived from God's call on your life. That means you understand that God has spoken to you and called you both to salvation and to a purpose in life. In the beginning, you may be the only person who recognizes this. In fact, you may not immediately recognize it yourself. Nevertheless, you will eventually become thoroughly convinced that the divine mark and seal of destiny is upon your life and ministry. There can be no spiritual authority without a calling from God.

THE CALLING

God has always spoken directly to individuals, beginning with Adam and continuing to the present day. Each of us may receive the call of God differently, and it may take time to recognize. Samuel, the great leader of God's people who anointed both King Saul and King David, heard God's call when he was just a small boy. When Samuel heard God's voice late one night, he thought it was the old priest Eli calling out to him. When he asked Eli about it, the elder man wisely understood that the boy was having neither a dream nor a hallucination but was receiving a calling from God. Eli instructed Samuel to respond to God's voice saying, "Speak, Lord; for thy servant heareth" (1 Sam. 3:9). The boy did exactly that and embarked on a long career as a prophet, priest, and kingmaker.

When you hear the voice of God, it may not be an audible voice such as Samuel heard. The Holy Ghost may come upon you with great power, giving you a revelation through a vision or dream. Or you may hear the still, small voice of God within your spirit. In any case, your response should be the same as Samuel's: "Speak, Lord. I'm ready and willing for whatever you have to say to me." As you pray, seek, and wait for God to speak, be patient. It took Samuel three times to truly hear and understand the voice of God. In time, you will come to recognize both God's way of speaking to you and the work that he has appointed you to do.

Has God spoken to you? Are you aware of the ways in which God communicates with your spirit? How have you responded? And what did God ask of you? That brings us to the next aspect of calling: *purpose*.

PURPOSE

We have already discovered the power of knowing your purpose in motivating you to pursue growth and in keeping you focused. You must realize also that your purpose is a result of your calling, not something that you choose for yourself. When God calls a person, he always gives him or her a mission—something to do. Your purpose is not rooted in your own will or ambition but in the will of God. That gives you spiritual authority for the work that you do.

While the calling and purpose originate with God, it is true that God calls people to do the things they delight in doing. Sometimes people fear listening for God's voice or accepting his calling because they fear it will lead them to something completely contrary to their abilities and desires. While God's calling is often a challenge, he normally calls us to the very things that we find great satisfaction in doing, though we may not realize that at the moment we are called. What do you believe God has called you to do? Have you discovered your purpose, or are you still seeking it? How have you responded to God's call? Do you feel timid or incapable of doing what God asks? That brings us to the next element of God's call: *gifting*.

GIFTING

God wants us to succeed in the mission he has for us. He wants us to be good at what we are called to do. You will have limitations, of course, but God will empower you to accomplish whatever he calls you to do. There is no calling without gifting. This is how Paul describes it in Ephesians 4:7, 11–15:

> *But unto every one of us is given grace according to the measure of the gift of Christ . . . And he gave some, apostles; and some, prophets; and some, evangelists; and some, pastors and teachers; For the perfecting of the saints, for the work of the ministry, for the edifying of the body of Christ: Till we all come in the unity of the faith, and of the knowledge of the Son of God, unto a perfect man, unto the measure of the stature of the fullness of Christ: That*

we henceforth be no more children, tossed to and fro, and carried about with every wind of doctrine, by the sleight of men, and cunning craftiness, whereby they lie in wait to deceive; But speaking the truth in love, may grow up into him in all things, which is the head, even Christ.

God wants all people to reach their full potential and he has given each of us a role to play in that process—a purpose. And he has gifted each of us to play that role perfectly. When you have a gift, others will recognize it and speak into your life. They will then benefit from that gift as it grows in you. We are all called in different areas that work together in the body and should not feel that we have to do more than our measure of faith. We can accept our limitations and learn to be the best at what God calls us to do. Has God called you? Then he has gifted you. Do you recognize your gifting? Whom can you ask to help you discover the gifts that God has given you?

When you accept the call of God on your life, it catapults you into a place where you will be used by God on a level others will not be. Your calling is the basis of your spiritual authority. When you have been called by God, you have divine permission—divine authority—to act. This spiritual authority is yours as a member of the body of Christ. As Peter put it, "But ye are a chosen generation, a royal priesthood, an holy nation, a peculiar people; that ye should shew forth the praises of him who hath called you out of darkness into his marvellous light" (1 Peter 2:9). Accept God's calling, accept your spiritual authority, and be a blessing in the lives of others.

LEVEL 2: CHARACTER

Spiritual authority is strengthened by good character.

The second level of spiritual authority is *character*. Spiritual authority is strengthened through good character. This is the level at which your life begins to match your calling. To have spiritual authority, your inner and outer life must be the same. Your words and actions much match the authority that you claim in Christ. This is why Paul writes so emphatically, "I therefore, the prisoner of the Lord, beseech you that ye walk worthy of the vocation wherewith ye are called" (Eph. 4:1). When your character grows to match your calling, your spiritual authority grows. When your character fails to match your calling, your spiritual authority is eroded. As former U.S. senator Alan K. Simpson put it, "If you have integrity, nothing else matters. If you don't have integrity, nothing else matters."[1]

Jesus pointed out the character issue in the Pharisees of his day. They claimed spiritual authority but lacked the character to go with it. Christ's indictment of them was withering:

> *The scribes and the Pharisees sit in Moses' seat: All therefore whatsoever they bid you observe, that observe and do; but do not ye after their works: for they say, and do not. For they bind heavy burdens and grievous to be borne, and lay them on men's shoulders; but they themselves will not move them with one of their fingers . . .*
>
> *Woe unto you, scribes and Pharisees, hypocrites! for ye make clean the outside of the cup and of the platter, but within they are full of extortion and excess. Thou blind Pharisee, cleanse first that which is*

within the cup and platter, that the outside of them may be clean also. (Matt. 23: 2–4, 25–26)

How closely does your character match your calling? Are you living up to the grace you have received? Could anyone truthfully apply the label *hypocrite* to you? If so, your spiritual authority will be weakened to the point of ineffectiveness. Let your good character strengthen your spiritual authority.

LEVEL 3: COMMITMENT

Spiritual authority depends on full commitment.

The third level of spiritual authority is *commitment*. Your spiritual authority depends on full commitment to your calling. After you have made the lifestyle changes that will bring your character in line with your calling, you must commit yourself fully to your purpose in Jesus Christ. You must recognize the obstacles in your way but maintain the perseverance needed to keep going. If you cannot get through the tough times, you will lose spiritual authority. Everybody wants to wear the crown, but few want to drink from the cup. Commitment is the willingness to carry your cross, drink from the cup—to share in the suffering of Christ so that you may also share in his glory. I want you to experience the crown, and that means learning to choose the right things in this life and remain committed to them. When you rise up and break the obstacles, your spiritual authority will be strengthened.

VISION VS. COMMITMENT

One reason people fail to remain committed to their calling is that they confuse vision with commitment. Vision is the picture of your preferred future. That's the destination you're headed for, and vision is always inspiring. Vision is what gets us out of bed in the morning. It is exciting to think about God's call on our lives and what we will accomplish as a result of it. Commitment, however, is something different. Commitment is your determination to achieve the vision, regardless of how long it may take, and your willingness to pay the price to get there. Vision says, "I believe this is what God has called me to do." Commitment says, "I will keep pushing until I get there, even when it's no fun anymore." John C. Maxwell expressed the difference this way: "Motivation gets you going, commitment keeps you growing."[2] What inspires you about your calling? What motivates you? Have you made a full commitment to pursue that goal, no matter the cost?

NO MATTER WHAT

Sooner or later your commitment will be tested. If you lack full commitment—that is, if you are keeping one foot in both worlds, pursuing God's calling and pursuing your own agenda—that will become apparent. The apostle James said, "A double minded man is unstable in all his ways" (James 1:8). Without commitment, you cannot stay the course to reach your full potential.

Becky Zerbe discovered the difference between calling and commitment in the context of marriage when Roger, her husband of many years, was diagnosed with early onset Alzheimer's disease. The couple was in the habit of journaling together, and their journal during those days became a cherished record of thoughts and fears during the progress of a life consuming illness. As the disease progressed, Roger wondered if their marriage commitment would weather the storm of his illness. After a particularly troubling bout of forgetfulness, Becky noted that her husband had written these words in the journal they shared:

Honey,

Today fear is taking over. The day is coming when all my memories of this life we share will be gone. In fact, you and the boys will be gone from me. I will lose you even as I am surrounded by you and your love. I don't want to leave you. I want to grow old in the warmth of memories. Forgive me for leaving so slowly and painfully.

Blinking back tears, Becky picked up her pen and wrote this reply:

My sweet husband,

What will happen when we get to the point where you no longer know me? I will continue to go on loving you and caring for you—not because you know me or remember our life, but because I remember you. I will remember the man who proposed to me and told me he loved me, the look on his face when his children were born, the father he was, the way he loved our extended family. I'll recall his love for riding, hiking, and reading, his tears at sentimental movies, the unexpected witty remarks, and how he held my hand while he prayed. I cherish the pleasure, obligation, commitment, and opportunity to care for you because I remember you.[8]

Spiritual authority must be backed to a commitment to keep going, no matter what. Spiritual authority gives you the ability to rule, to overcome, and to transform the bitter into something sweet. To exercise that authority, you need commitment to the vision and purpose of God for your life.

Commitment adds to your authority, just as it did to Joshua when he stood before the Israelites and declared: "Choose you this day whom ye will serve; whether the gods which your fathers served that were on the other side of the flood, or the gods of the Amorites, in whose land ye dwell: but as for me and my house, we will serve the Lord" (Josh. 24:15). Because he was willing to put both feet in, he had the spiritual authority to lead. When your calling is backed up by commitment, you will weather any obstacle. Your spiritual authority will grow stronger as you keep the faith.

What is challenging you right now? What is it that makes you feel weary or ready to give up? Press on. You have a calling, a gifting, and your character will not allow you to quit.

LEVEL 4: CONSISTENCY

Spiritual authority grows by consistent action.

The fourth level of spiritual authority is *consistency*. Spiritual authority grows by consistent action. When you learn to operate by faith rather than feelings, you gain authority. When you are not able to master your emotions, giving in to volatile feelings that can come with victory or defeat, opposition or applause, you lose spiritual authority.

WHAT CONSISTENCY LOOKS LIKE

Two biblical figures offer clear examples of the level of consistency. One is a negative example, and the other is a positive one. Let's begin with the negative example, King Saul. Saul was one of the weakest leaders in the Bible, in part because he was completely unable to master his emotions. Though he had been anointed as king and invested with spiritual authority, he was not able to reach the level of consistency. He was alternatively bold and timid, cruel and kind, obedient and disobedient, devoted and faithless. At one point, the Bible records, "But the Spirit of the Lord departed from Saul, and an evil spirit from the Lord troubled him" (1 Sam. 16:14). At that point Saul's emotions became even more volatile than ever. As a result, God removed him as king and appointed David in his place. Because he was never able to reach the level of consistency, Saul lost all spiritual authority. In the end, he took his own life after losing a pivotal battle with the Philistines (1 Sam. 31:4).

Contrast Saul's life with the positive example of Daniel, a man of great spiritual authority. Daniel lived during the period when the Jewish people were exiled in Babylon. He was a highly competent leader and was promoted to a position of great responsibility by the Persian king, Darius. Daniel was a man of great faith, as his consistent habit of daily prayer demonstrated. However, Daniel's enemies conspired to use that very faith against him by encouraging Darius to pass a law stating that no one could pray to anyone but the king for thirty days. Anyone who broke that law would be thrown to the lions. How would Daniel respond? Would he remain consistent in character, or would he give in to fear?

Here's what happened: "Now when Daniel knew that the writing was signed, he went into his house; and his windows being open in his chamber toward Jerusalem, he kneeled upon his knees three times a day, and prayed, and gave thanks before his God, as he did aforetime" (Dan. 6:10). Not even the threat of being torn apart by lions could deter Daniel. His actions remained consistent, regardless of the circumstances. He stands to this day as an example of great spiritual authority.

TAKING CONTROL OF YOUR EMOTIONS

The further you progress in spiritual authority, the higher the stakes will be. That makes it imperative to take authority over your mind and heart, and especially your emotions. Do not allow the constantly shifting circumstances of your life to affect your commitment. You should not be in a different mood every time you come to church. Gather for worship with confidence that God will move, regardless of how you feel. Do not allow your passions to take control of you, leading you to do things you know are inconsistent with your character. Make choices based on your deepest values, not your temporary feelings. When you continue to pursue your full potential regardless of your emotional state, you increase your productivity and the possibility for success.

This is not a matter of faking it or pretending things that you do not feel. Consistency is not acting as if you do not have emotions. Instead, it is choosing to be mature and behave consistently regardless of how you feel in any given moment. People who are inconsistent cannot function unless their feelings exactly match their actions. They pursue God's calling when it feels good to do so. However, when they feel anger or frustration or lethargy, they cannot help but act on those negative urges. To have spiritual authority, you must learn to function consistently, based on faith, regardless of your feelings.

CHOOSING TO WALK IN THE SPIRIT

To gain the upper hand on your feelings, ground your thinking in the reality of God's Word. Remember these words from the apostle Paul:

> *There is therefore now no condemnation to them which are in Christ Jesus, who walk not after the flesh, but after the Spirit. For the law of the Spirit of life in Christ Jesus hath made me free from the law of sin and death. For what the law could not do, in that it was weak through the flesh, God sending his own Son in the likeness of sinful flesh, and for sin, condemned sin in the flesh: That the righteousness of the law might be fulfilled in us, who walk not after the flesh, but after the Spirit. (Rom. 8:1–4)*

Choose to act on what you know to be real—your standing with Christ as a new person—and not on feelings, which are so uncertain and changeable. Choose to cooperate with the Holy Spirit, who lives within you. When you do, your actions will be consistent, and your spiritual authority will grow. Calling plus character plus commitment will lead you to consistency.

What situations make you emotional or anxious? Is there a particular emotion, such as loneliness or anger or self-pity, to which you are especially susceptible? Ground your thinking in Scripture. Claim the promises of Christ, and step forward in faith. This is the pathway to spiritual authority.

LEVEL 5: CONVICTION

Spiritual authority resonates from a heart of conviction.

The fifth level of spiritual authority is *conviction*. Spiritual authority resonates from a heart of conviction. If you passionately believe that what you are doing is God's purpose in your life, you will be highly effective. If you succumb to doubt or lack passion in your faith, you will lack spiritual authority as well. Great faith brings great spiritual authority.

PASSION VS. PERFORMANCE

Many people fail to rise to the highest level of spiritual authority because their pursuit of God's calling is merely a performance, not the result of true passion. What's the difference? Performance is based on a script; it is doing exactly what you are supposed to do, no more and no less. Passion leads to spontaneous acts that may go above and beyond what is required based on an inner joy or drive. Performance is going through the motions, doing things you don't truly want to do because you believe you have to. Passion is doing the exact same things but with joy, energy, and motivation. The Pharisees were performers. They did exactly what was required, but their hearts did not truly align with God's purpose. Jesus had passion. He sometimes broke the rules, but everything he did exhibited his overwhelming desire to please the Father. You may be in the right place doing the right thing at the right time, but if you lack passion you are just going through the motions and have no spiritual authority. Authority rises from your conviction that you are doing exactly what God intends for you to do—and doing it with all your heart.

THE POWER OF FAITH

Conviction elevates your actions into a new level of authority that will affect heaven, move earth, and lift you to the place that God's purpose has desired for you. This firm faith is exactly what God wants to see in each of us, as the writer of Hebrews shows: "But without faith it is impossible to please him: for he that cometh to God must believe that he is, and that he is a rewarder of them that diligently seek him" (Heb. 11:6). When we have this kind of conviction, we have great spiritual authority and anything is possible. Hebrews 11 goes on to tell the incredible exploits of biblical heroes who had true conviction:

> *And what shall I more say? for the time would fail me to tell of Gedeon, and of Barak, and of Samson, and of Jephthae; of David also, and Samuel, and of the prophets: Who through faith subdued kingdoms, wrought righteousness, obtained promises, stopped the mouths of lions. Quenched the violence of fire, escaped the edge of the sword, out of weakness were made strong, waxed valiant in fight, turned to flight the armies of the aliens. Women received their dead raised to life again: and others were tortured, not accepting deliverance; that they might obtain a better resurrection: And others had trial of cruel mockings and scourgings, yea, moreover of bonds and imprisonment: They were stoned, they were sawn asunder, were tempted, were slain with the sword: they wandered about in sheepskins and goatskins; being destitute, afflicted, tormented; (Of whom the world was not worthy:) they wandered in deserts, and in mountains, and in dens and caves of the earth. (Heb. 11:32–38)*

These people, and many more like them, achieved amazing things through faith. They had great spiritual authority because they had great conviction. Nothing was impossible for them. And the same will be true for you. Those who are *sold out* can never be *bought out*. You already have all that you need to achieve your full potential: you have the calling, gifting, and purpose of God upon your life. You have spiritual authority to grow and lead others in growing. This is the time to trust God like never before and give your very best. Rise up and take the authority that has been given to you in Christ!

GROWTH ACTIVITIES

You have been given spiritual authority based on your calling. God has specifically invited you not only to be part of his family through salvation but also to take part in his mission through his purpose and gifting. Reaching your full potential means growing into that spiritual authority through the five levels: calling, character, commitment, consistency, and conviction. Here are three simple activities that will help you grow in the spiritual authority you have been given.

WRITE AND SHARE YOUR TESTIMONY

Spiritual authority begins with God's call on your life. God has been present and active in your life since before you were born. He has been speaking to you in ways you may not have recognized at first. By writing your testimony, you will identify God's call more clearly and gain a more definite picture of your purpose. Begin by creating a timeline of your life. First, draw a horizontal line on a sheet of paper, representing your life from birth to the present. On that line, make a mark for each significant life event and label it. Then make a mark for each significant spiritual event and label it. Finally, write your faith story, highlighting the ways that God has spoken to you or confirmed his word to you throughout your life. End with a written statement of your life's purpose. Share this testimony with at least one person, and it will strengthen your conviction.

ENLIST AN ACCOUNTABILITY PARTNER

To help you grow in character, enlist an accountability partner. The function of an accountability partner differs from that of a Growth Team, though there are some similarities. An accountability partner will hold you accountable for specific areas of your life that you ask him or her to check up on and pray for. This person will help you develop character by working with you on your weak spots. You accountability partner must be:

- A person of the same gender as you.
- Someone who is serious about growing to his or her full potential.
- Trustworthy, mature, and able to keep confidences.
- Willing to meet with you at least biweekly by phone or in person for conversation, coaching, and prayer.

Ideally, your accountability relationship will be a two-way street, meaning that you will also provide accountability for your partner. You will grow together in character and spiritual authority.

SELECT A MENTOR

A mentor is different from an accountability partner in that a mentor is further advanced in spiritual authority and able to act as a guide. Generally, a mentor will be someone older than yourself and several levels beyond you in authority. A mentoring relationship can be formal or informal, meaning that you can make this an explicit relationship in which you meet periodically to ask questions and seek advice, or it may be an informal relationship in which you observe and casually interact with your mentor. Pastors, teachers, mature saints, and leaders are all possible mentors. Also, your mentor does not have to be alive! You can receive mentoring through the writings of great leaders from other eras. Choose a person who has progressed beyond you in spiritual authority and learn all you can from that person.

You already have what you need to reach your full potential—the calling, purpose, and gifting of God. You have both his permission and authority to grow and lead others in growing. As you develop greater spiritual authority, you will become more mature, faith decisions will become easier, and you will be able to help others reach their full potential also. You don't need anyone's permission to transform your life and your world. You have God's full authority, and that is more than enough!

ACTION LIST

1. Write your personal testimony and share it with your Growth Team.

2. Name three potential accountability partners and contact the first on your list to schedule a meeting.

3. Take a character inventory, listing your top three personal strengths and top three areas of vulnerability.

4. Select a mentor and list three things you would like to learn from that person.

5. Share Strategy No. 3: Take Spiritual Authority with one person today.

STRATEGY NO. 4

Seek Divine Favor

Your Ability to Lead is Determined by Your Capacity to Grow

For whosoever hath, to him shall be given, and he shall have more abundance: but whosoever hath not, from him shall be taken away even that he hath.
—*Matthew 13:12*

Warren Buffett is one of the wealthiest people in the world. The octogenarian investor from Omaha, Nebraska, holds personal assets estimated at $67.3 billion.[1] Buffett made headlines when he announced that he would give $31 billion of his fortune to fund the Bill and Melinda Gates Foundation's work in fighting infectious diseases and reforming education.[2] He's been making good on that pledge ever since, having donated over $15 billion to the foundation in eight years.[3] Many people find that generosity admirable, but perhaps even more people are interested in knowing how Buffett made his fortune in the first place. Was it wisdom, good fortune, or plain old hard work that enabled a Midwestern boy to rise from selling chewing gum door to door to being the third richest person in the world? The answer is surprisingly simple. Here is Buffet's investment strategy in his own words:

> *I look for something that I can understand to start with; there are all kinds of businesses I don't understand. I don't understand what car companies are going to do ten years from now, or what software or chemical companies are going to do ten years from now, but I do understand that Snickers bars will be the number one candy company in the U.S.—like it's been for forty years. So, I look for durable competitive advantage, and that is hard to find. I look for an honest and able management, and I look for the price I'm going to pay.*[4]

So there it is. Identify a well-run company that has an advantage over the competition and invest in it at a reasonable price. In other words, find someone who has proven they are already good at making money, and give them some of yours.

That simple advice seems to have worked for the man who has been dubbed the Oracle of Omaha. Class A stock in his holding company, Berkshire Hathaway, is the most expensive of any publicly held U.S. company, valued at over $200,000. With dozens of subsidiaries, including in railroads, insurance and energy, Berkshire Hathaway posted $182 billion in revenue in a recent year with $19.5 billion in net income.[5]

Buffett's story is a wonderful tale of financial success, but it is more than that. This modest man's simple investment strategy is a powerful example, in a temporal way, of a spiritual concept; Strategy No. 4: *Seek Divine Favor.* Your ability to lead is determined by your capacity to grow. What has been true for Buffett and many others in financial terms is true for you spiritually as well. Once you begin to grow, you will gain opportunities for further growth and leadership. Your growth will fuel itself.

In financial terms, that is easy to understand. People who are successful tend to become more successful over time. Companies that make a profit tend to get larger and stronger, while companies that struggle tend to continue struggling or go out of business. Whatever causes the company to do well—its durable competitive advantage, to use Buffett's term—multiplies over time. Success breeds success.

In spiritual terms, growth breeds growth. When you begin to grow toward your full potential, you are more likely to keep growing. As Jesus put it, "For whosoever hath, to him shall be given, and he shall have more abundance: but whosoever hath not, from him shall be taken away even that he hath" (Matt. 13:12). Those who invest their spiritual authority will grow toward their full potential. When they do, they will receive even more spiritual authority. They will have greater opportunities, greater wisdom, and greater *favor* with God. And that favor will result in even more growth.

The divine favor works in reverse too. Those who do not use their spiritual authority will lose it. Even what they have will be taken from them, and they'll be less likely to reach their full potential. That makes it vital to understand and practice this concept. When you grow in one area, you'll likely grow in other areas. When you apply yourself to reaching your full potential, your growth will accelerate. When you invest your spiritual authority in growing yourself and leading others, you will succeed.

However, if you fail to be diligent, you won't remain in place. You will actually fall back from where you are.

Let's explore divine favor further using the very best life example, that of Jesus Christ. For Luke tells us that as a young boy, "Jesus increased in wisdom and stature, and in favour with God and man" (Luke 2:52). Even as a child, Jesus possessed tremendous spiritual authority. As he grew intellectually, physically, and relationally, he also grew in favor with the Father. This is the divine in action. We will examine what that looks like in each of the four critical areas mentioned in the life of Jesus:

- Wisdom
- Stature
- Favor with God
- Favor with Others

Then we will identify practical ideas for seeking divine favor in your life. When we are through, you will have a clear action plan for taking the next steps toward reaching your full potential. If you discipline yourself and apply growth principles to these four areas of your life, your growth will multiply and you will reach your full potential as the leader and minister that God has called you to be.

GROWTH IN WISDOM

You must learn to apply God's will to every area of your life.

The first area in which you must grow in order to experience divine favor is *wisdom*. To grow in wisdom, you must learn to apply God's will to every area of your life. Dr. Larry Lea defines wisdom as "the God-given ability to perceive the true nature of a matter and to implement the will of God in that matter."[6] You will be faced with many decisions regarding your ministry, your family, your job, your friends, and your finances. Each of these decisions represents a crossroads in your life. To navigate them successfully, you will need wisdom.

The most dangerous intersection in the United States during a recent two-year period was the corner of Flamingo Road and Pines Boulevard in Pembroke Pines, Florida, located north of Miami. That is according to a report from State Farm Insurance. During that time, 357 crashes were reported at the intersection, which is bordered by three malls and the C. B. Smith Park. According to State Farm, nearly ninety thousand cars pass through the intersection each day, resulting in an average of one accident about every other day. Those accidents resulted in property damage totaling over one million dollars for each of the years studied.[7] Like a south Florida driver heading for the mall, you will pass through many dangerous intersections on your journey to full maturity. There is the intersection of your personal ambitions and the call of God, and the junction of your personal desires and your vows to faithfulness. You will pass through the crossroads of financial pressure and personal integrity. If you are to grow to full potential, you will need wisdom to navigate each of these dangerous interchanges. In other words, you must be able to recognize the true nature of the situation you face and be able to apply God's will to it.

Our best example of biblical wisdom is King Solomon. Shortly after Solomon was crowned king of Israel, succeeding his father, the legendary King David, the Lord appeared to Solomon in a dream and made a unique offer—the only one of its kind so far as we know. God said to the young king, "Ask what I shall give thee" (1 Kings 3:5). In other words, God offered to grant any request to Solomon. His response shows that he already had a healthy dose of what he would ask for. Solomon responded: "And now, O Lord my God, thou hast made thy servant king instead of David my father: and I am but a little child: I know not how to go out or come in. And thy servant is in the midst of thy people which thou hast chosen, a great people, that cannot be numbered nor counted for multitude. Give therefore thy servant an understanding heart to judge thy people, that I may discern between good and bad: for who is able to judge this thy so great a people?" (1 Kings 3:7–9).

Even as a king, Solomon recognized the need for wisdom. We, as leaders, need to understand the responsibilities that come with that role and recognize the need to ask God for the wisdom both to live faithful lives and to influence others. Proverbs 4:7 advises us of the importance of wisdom: "Wisdom is the principal thing; therefore get wisdom: and with all thy getting get understanding." As we look further into the Word of God, James gives us proper instructions on how to receive this wisdom: "If any of you lack wisdom, let him ask of God, that giveth to all men liberally, and upbraideth not; and it shall be given him" (James 1:5).

Because Solomon's request pleased the Lord, he also bestowed upon him riches and honor. When you, as a leader, follow the biblical principle of wisdom, honor will follow. This is the divine favor in action.

There are times, of course, when the best exercise of wisdom is not to navigate difficult intersections but to avoid them entirely. Bill Curry, former head football coach at Georgia State University and ESPN analyst, played ten seasons as a center in the National

Football League, including winning two Super Bowls, one with the Green Bay Packers and another with the then Baltimore Colts. However, when Vince Lombardi drafted Curry in 1965, he was convinced he wouldn't make the team without a competitive edge. Prior to tryouts, the young athlete began taking steroids and bulked up from 220 to 240 pounds in a very short time.

When Curry's father noticed the remarkable improvement, Curry said, "It's just incredible what these pills can do, Dad!" At that, his father took the pills, walked to the bathroom, and poured them down the toilet. The younger man got flustered, thinking he would never make the team. "What are you doing?" he asked. In reply, Curry's father warned him about the danger of steroid abuse and how it would eventually damage his body. Curry was shaken but convinced, and he quit using the drug. Today he simply says, "I'm so glad I had a father who loved me like that."

You have a heavenly Father who loves you enough to warn you about the things you ought to avoid: sexual immorality, drunkenness, untruthfulness, materialism, gossip. That's a partial list, of course. For more examples of the things you would be wise to avoid, try reading Galatians 5:19–21 or Ephesians 5:3–20. Wisdom means listening to those warnings and choosing to stay well away from the influences and practices that will erode your spiritual authority, sap your growth, and result in losing rather than gaining favor.

Do you need wisdom? You need only to ask your heavenly Father for it. If you are facing a difficult crossroads right now, seek wisdom from the Lord. He wants you to succeed in reaching your full potential. Learn to see reality as it is and apply God's will to every situation in your life.

GROWTH IN STATURE

You must grow to maturity in Christ.

The second area in which you must grow in order to experience the divine favor is *stature*. To grow in stature, you must move to full maturity in Christ. Stature can have two meanings. The first is the physical height of a person when standing upright. As applied to Jesus, this is undoubtedly one meaning of the term. The boy Jesus grew into Jesus the man—he grew larger. However, stature has a second meaning and this applies as well. Stature also means the status or standing of a person gained as a result of growth (not necessarily physical growth) or achievement. Stature is synonymous with reputation, name, character, or standing among others. Undoubtedly, Jesus also grew in this way. He gained a reputation, or name, as he grew in wisdom. You, too, will grow in stature as you move toward your full potential. This is an important aspect of divine favor.

Leonard Ravenhill, the renowned British evangelist, was fond of telling stories. He reportedly told one about a group of tourists visiting a picturesque village who walked by an old man sitting beside a fence. In a patronizing way, one tourist asked, "Were any great men born in this village?" The old man replied, "Nope, only babies." Most of us would like to think that achieving full stature happens instantly, or at least quickly. But it does not. Growing to full stature takes time. But if you apply the necessary biblical principles and work diligently, you will grow into the stature of the fullness of Christ. The apostle Paul outlines that process in Ephesians 4:11–16:

> *And he gave some, apostles; and some, prophets; and some, evangelists; and some, pastors and teach-*

> ers; For the perfecting of the saints, for the work of the ministry, for the edifying of the body of Christ: Till we all come in the unity of the faith, and of the knowledge of the Son of God, unto a perfect man, unto the measure of the stature of the fullness of Christ: That we henceforth be no more children, tossed to and fro, and carried about with every wind of doctrine, by the sleight of men, and cunning craftiness, whereby they lie in wait to deceive; But speaking the truth in love, may grow up into him in all things, which is the head, even Christ: From whom the whole body fitly joined together and compacted by that which every joint supplieth, according to the effectual working in the measure of every part, maketh increase of the body unto the edifying of itself in love.

As we build one another up, we grow to become fully mature in Christ, not lacking in anything. Then we are better able to resist the temptations and pressures of the world. We come to actually live like Jesus. The apostle Peter said something almost identical in 2 Peter 1:3–8. Watch the progression in these verses, and pay close attention to the very first line:

> According as his divine power hath given unto us all things that pertain unto life and godliness, through the knowledge of him that hath called us to glory and virtue: Whereby are given unto us exceeding great and precious promises: that by these ye might be partakers of the divine nature, having escaped the corruption that is in the world through

> lust. *And beside this, giving all diligence, add to your faith virtue; and to virtue knowledge; And to knowledge temperance; and to temperance patience; and to patience godliness; And to godliness brotherly kindness; and to brotherly kindness charity. For if these things be in you, and abound, they make you that ye shall neither be barren nor unfruitful in the knowledge of our Lord Jesus Christ.*

First, we see here the strategy of taking spiritual authority—you already have what you need in order to grow! Peter also speaks of divine favor, showing that when we add virtue to our lives, we move from one growth point to the next with ever-increasing momentum. As a result, we become fruitful in Christ—we reach our full potential!

Do not make the mistake of taking your stature for granted. You have been given a new standing as a child of God, but you must live up to that new name. Sadly, not everyone does. In 1958 a man named Robert Lane had a son whom he gave the whimsical name of Winner. Perhaps the elder Lane hoped the name would be a self-fulfilling prophecy. Who could fail in life with a name like Winner Lane?

Some years later, the Lanes had another son. This one, Robert Lane gave the dubious name Loser. With a name like that, you can imagine that the younger Lane boy had many challenges in life. Here is where the story gets really interesting. Despite his unappealing name, Loser Lane succeeded in life. He graduated from college and later became a sergeant with the New York Police Department. No one there calls him Loser. His coworkers refer to him as Lou. Oddly, Winner Lane has not done well in life. He has a long criminal record with nearly three dozen arrests for crimes including burglary, domestic violence, trespassing, and resisting arrest.[9]

It isn't enough to claim a change of identity. You must grow into that identity; you must live up to your new name. That's what it means to grow in stature. A growing faith is not accidental but intentional. You must take the necessary steps to maturity in your life. You don't fall into leadership; you must grow into leadership. Where are you growing in stature? Where do you need to grow? How would you assess your current level of maturity? What would it take for you to move to another level in maturity?

GROWTH IN FAVOR WITH GOD

You must live faithfully according to God's word.

The third area in which you must grow in order to experience the divine favor is *favor with God*. To grow in favor with God, you must live faithfully according to God's Word. Favor with God is a right standing with God that results in blessing. This is not a material blessing but is a spiritual blessing from God, which often involves a call to serve. When you answer God's call, the divine favor allows you to be called to ever-higher levels of service.

We see this clearly in the life of Mary, who found favor with God and was chosen to give birth to the Son of God. "And the angel came in unto her, and said, Hail, thou that art highly favoured, the Lord is with thee: blessed art thou among women" (Luke 1:28). Mary was a humble, obedient servant and therefore found favor with God. As a result, she was chosen for an even greater honor. She gained divine favor.

In a remarkable parallel to Luke 2:52, we see this principle illustrated in the life of Samuel as well: "And the child Samuel grew on, and was in favour both with the LORD, and also with men" (1 Sam. 2:26). The young boy Samuel grew in the very same ways that Jesus did, and he, too, was given the honor of serving in a high capacity, as a prophet and judge of Israel.

So how does one gain favor with God? What was it about Mary and Samuel and so many other biblical heroes that caused God to be especially pleased with them? A number of Bible passages tell us plainly that God's favor comes from living faithfully according to God's Word. Let's review a few of them.

Psalms 1:1–3 states: "Blessed is the man that walketh not in the counsel of the ungodly, nor standeth in the way of sinners, nor sitteth in the seat of the scornful. But his delight is in the law of the Lord; and in his law doth he meditate day and night. And he shall be like a tree planted by the rivers of water, that bringeth forth his fruit in his season; his leaf also shall not wither; and whatsoever he doeth shall prosper." Interestingly, Psalm 1 is known as a *wisdom psalm* because it gives practical advice for living. So growth in wisdom, or applying God's truth to the situations in your life, results in favor. Are you walking daily in God's Word, living faithfully according to it?

Proverbs 12:22 says, "Lying lips are an abomination to the LORD, but they that deal truly are his delight." God is pleased with those who have integrity; that is, with those whose words and actions match. Lying or any form of deceitfulness always displeases God. Those who find favor with him are transparent, honest, forthright, and trustworthy. How closely do your words and actions match? Are you known for being a person of integrity? How might you grow in this area?

In 1 Samuel 15:22, Samuel said, "Hath the LORD as great delight in burnt offerings and sacrifices, as in obeying the voice of the LORD? Behold, to obey is better than sacrifice, and to hearken than the fat of rams." In other words, God finds favor with those who obey his Word rather than those who are simply remorseful about their disobedience—or, worse yet, who make a show of their religious observances without really intending to obey. Are you obedient to the known will of God for your life? Do you live faithfully according to his Word? Are you growing in obedience so that you are less likely to be beset by the same temptations and sins?

The prophet Micah states in Micah 6:8: "He hath shewed thee, O man, what is good; and what doth the LORD require of thee, but to do justly, and to love mercy, and to walk humbly with thy God?" God delights in those who act justly and love mercy, which means that they treat others fairly, are honest in all their dealings, and do not allow injustice to stand. God has a special place in his heart for the weak, often identified in Scripture as "the fatherless and widows" (see James 1:27 for one example of this). In reality, God cares about all helpless people and will not tolerate their mistreatment. Those who stand up for the weak find favor with God. So our growth to full potential depends on ministry, not only to other people but to the Lord as well.

Are you growing in favor with God? To do so, you must live faithfully according to his Word. When you begin to seek divine favor, the blessing of the Lord will come upon you and you will be called to higher levels of responsibility. What would it take for you to grow in the area of favor with God?

GROW IN FAVOR WITH OTHERS

To grow in favor with others, you must serve them.

The fourth area in which you must grow in order to experience divine favor is *favor with others*. To grow in favor with others, you must serve them. We often think of favor with others as a kind of fame or popularity that allows us to receive something *from* others. But remember that "God so loved the world that he gave"! Saved people serve people. We find favor with other people by offering something *to* them. As you grow in your service to others, divine favor will come into play and you will find yourself receiving greater opportunities to serve and grow.

We see favor through serving in Proverbs 3:3–4, which says, "Let not mercy and truth forsake thee: bind them about thy neck; write them upon the table of thine heart: So shalt thou find favour and good understanding in the sight of God and man." This verse is a strong parallel to John 1:14, where the apostle describes Jesus this way: "And the Word was made flesh, and dwelt among us, (and we beheld his glory, the glory as of the only begotten of the Father,) full of grace and truth." As we come to love mercy (or grace) and truth, meaning that we care about living out God's Word by caring for them and bringing gospel truth to them, we will grow in favor with others. Gaining favor with others is a product of the mercy shown to them and the truth that we adhere to and love. People may not always agree with you, but when your walk matches your speech, they will respect you. People know when they are loved.

Mother Teresa embodied the concept of favor with others as few others have. This woman, who devoted her life to serving the poor and dying on the streets of one of India's most populous cities, was largely unknown outside Calcutta until she was "discovered" by the English journalist Malcom Muggeridge. Muggeridge was a well-known media personality during the later twentieth century. And he was controversial—known in earlier life as a heavy drinker and womanizer. So when the playboy journalist from Britain descended to the slums of India to interview Mother Teresa, he was rather full of himself and his own ideas.

After only a few days of watching her interact with dying people at the hospice she operated, the journalist was bold enough to offer advice. He told Mother Teresa that she was wasting her time with most of the children she treated. Muggeridge pointed out that many of them would die no matter what she did, so she should just leave them alone. He further pointed out that other children were less seriously ill and therefore didn't require as much attention—she should ignore them too. It was the middle group, those who might survive with serious intervention, on which she should spend her time. In other words, Muggeridge said, she should practice triage.

Mother Teresa just looked at him. She paused for a moment. And then she said, "Mr. Muggeridge, let me ask you a question. What is the worst thing that could happen to a person?" Muggeridge fumbled for some politically correct answer, and Mother Teresa replied, "No, no. That's not it at all. The worst thing that could happen to a person is that they would be unloved." She went on to say:

> The first woman I saw I myself picked up from the street. She had been half eaten by the rats and ants. I took her to the hospital but they could not do anything for her. They only took her in because I

> *refused to move until they accepted her . . . Within twenty-four hours [after receiving a building from the city for use as our hospice] we had our patients there and we started the work of the home for the sick and dying who are destitutes. Since then we have picked up over twenty-three thousand people from the streets of Calcutta of which about fifty percent have died.*

Muggeridge responded: "What exactly are you doing for these dying people?"

Mother Teresa said, "First of all we want to make them feel that they are wanted, we want them to know that there are people who really love them, who really wanted them, at least for the few hours they have to live, to know human and divine love. That they too may know that they are the children of God, and that they are not forgotten and that they are loved and cared about and there are young lives ready to give themselves in their service."[10]

Malcom Muggeridge went back to England a changed man. He wrote the book, *Something Beautiful for God: Mother Teresa of Calcutta*, and within a short time, the unknown Albanian nun who had devoted her life to showing God's love to dying people became an international celebrity. And Malcolm Muggeridge became a convert to Christianity.

This is the power of finding favor with others. When we unselfishly serve, putting mercy into action but not forgetting truth, we gain the respect of others. We gain the ability to lead. Favor with others is not fame, though fame may accompany it. This is not popularity; in fact, it is just as likely to lead to being unpopular. Instead, favor with others is the respect that comes from loving others as Christ has loved us.

Your ability to lead is determined by your capacity to grow. When you grow, you find favor, and that favor propels you to greater opportunities, greater growth, and greater leadership. May you, by following the same path that Jesus took, merit the same commendation he received. It is not always an easy path, but it is worth every step. The hills you climb and the valleys you go through are not for your *de*struction; they are for your *con*struction. God uses our struggles, our wilderness experiences and valley experiences, to build us up into the leaders that he desires us to be.

GROWTH ACTIVITIES

When a child grows, that growth appears to be normal or unaided. After all, children do grow larger and begin to explore the world on their own. However, every parent knows that without some assistance and without the right conditions, a child will not thrive. You can foster your own growth in wisdom, stature, favor with God, and favor with others by creating the conditions and opportunities that you need in order to reach your full potential. As you do, you will grow in the ways we have discussed and begin to experience favor. Be creative, and remember Strategy No. 2, Accept Personal Responsibility: you are responsible for your own growth. Here are some practical steps to get you started on seeking divine favor.

PRACTICE THEOLOGICAL REFLECTION

To grow in wisdom, apply the practice of theological reflection to a problem or decision that you are facing. Though this sounds complicated, it is actually quite simple. Theological reflection is a way of thinking through a problem in order to find God's will in it. To do this, follow these steps. You may find it helpful to write down your responses.

Step 1: State the problem. Using objective language, state the problem, situation, or decision as clearly and simply as you can. Also state the crux of the problem, that is, why it poses a moral, ethical, or theological challenge.

Step 2: Analyze the problem biblically. List Bible passages that shed light on this problem or question and briefly summarize your findings.

Step 3: Analyze the problem theologically. Think about this problem in relation to what you know about the character of God. Summarize your thoughts.

Step 4: Analyze the problem ecclesiologically. That is, think about the problem in relation to what you know about the church, its traditions, its leadership and authority. Summarize your findings.

Step 5: Analyze the problem reflexively. This means thinking about your own thoughts, emotions, experiences, and feelings. Why do you feel as you do about this? Why is it a particular challenge for you? Summarize your feelings.

Step 6: Pray. Seriously seek God, asking for his wisdom, as James 1:5 advises.

Step 7: State your conclusions. Summarizing your reflections and adding the wisdom received through prayer, state what you believe to be God's will in this situation.

This is not a magic formula for determining the will of God, but the practice of theological reflection will help you sort through any circumstance from a variety of viewpoints and seek God's wisdom. What other activities can you think of that would help you develop wisdom, applying God's will to the situations in your life?

BEGIN A PEER MASTERMIND GROUP

To help you grow in stature, begin a *mastermind group*. A mastermind group is a small group of peers that meets intentionally for brainstorming, education, peer accountability, and support concerning some aspect of life or ministry. Your Growth Team is an example of a mastermind group, but you may wish to begin another to specifically work on some aspect of your life or ministry such as preaching, parenting, church leadership, or fundraising. A mastermind group is more focused than a small group, having a single growth or learning objective; but, like any good small group, it depends on commitment, confidentiality, willingness to give and receive support, respect, and honesty among its members. As you lead others in learning, setting goals, and achieving more together, you will gain stature with your peers. What other ideas can you think of for growing in stature? What hindrances do you see that would need to be overcome?

TAKE A PERSONAL RETREAT

To grow in favor with God, take a personal retreat for a minimum of twenty-four hours in order to pray, reflect on your life, and allow the Holy Ghost to point out any area in which you need greater obedience to the Word of God. This does not have to be expensive or highly structured. You could to this at a campground or retreat center, or at your own home. The key to this type of retreat is to withdraw from the company of others so that you can better hear the voice of God. Unplug electronically so that you will not be distracted by the phone, Internet, or social media. Plan time for rest, prayer, Scripture reading, reflection, and journaling. Your goal is to listen to the Spirit and apply the Word to your life. What other ways can you imagine to grow in favor with God; that is, to apply his Word more fully to your life?

GO ON A SHORT-TERM MISSION TRIP

To grow in favor with others, take on a significant service assignment such as a short-term mission trip. Some other possible acts of service could be volunteering at a pregnancy care center or homeless shelter, serving with an organization that assists with housing such as Habitat for Humanity or Christmas in Action, or volunteering at a hospital. Choose something that meets a genuine need for others and does not benefit you in any way—other than the blessing of serving. As you serve others selflessly, you will grow in stature and gain favor with others, both those you serve and the peers who will follow your example. What other activities might you do that would help you grow in favor with others?

Jesus is our example of growth in every way, and his life shows that your full potential is not a single-faceted jewel. You are a complex, complete person, and you must grow in every area in order to attain all that God has in store for you. Remember that your ability to lead is directly related to your ability and willingness to grow. And there is a snowball effect. The more you grow, the more you will want to grow and have opportunities to lead. That's the result of divine favor. And it works both ways. When you back off, your momentum slows down. I am confident of great things for you. You are beginning to grow in many ways. Keep going! God favors the work you are doing.

ACTION LIST

1. Take an inventory of yourself as regards your experience of divine favor. List the specific ways in which you would like to grow in wisdom, stature, favor with God, and favor with others.

2. Choose one growth activity for yourself in each of the four areas, and schedule when you will complete it.

3. Review the progress of your Growth Team to ensure that members are keeping accountable and the group is making progress; make any necessary midcourse corrections.

4. Review your action steps from the previous chapters. If you have not completed an action, consider the reasons why. Be honest with yourself. If you are avoiding growth in any area, spend time in prayer about that.

5. Tell someone about Strategy No. 4: Seek Divine Favor today.

STRATEGY NO. 5

Learn from Pain

Suffering Produces Growth

*Consider it pure joy, my brothers and sisters,
whenever you face trials of many kinds, because you
know that the testing of your faith produces perseverance.
Let perseverance finish its work so that you may be
mature and complete, not lacking anything.*
—James 1:2–4 NIV

Wang Mingdao was one of the best-known church leaders in China for most of the twentieth century. Though he had no formal theological training, Wang founded the Christian Tabernacle, a church that grew to become one of China's largest evangelical congregations during the 1940s. Wang also had an itinerant ministry throughout China, preaching in hundreds of churches of nearly all denominations. He was a prolific writer, and founded the Christian newspaper *Spiritual Food Quarterly*. By the late 1950s, Wang was approaching sixty years of age and at the height of his career as a pastor, evangelist, author, and teacher.

By all appearances, this humble, gifted, godly man had reached his full potential as a leader in Christ's church. Yet God had one more lesson in store for this dedicated servant.

In 1955 Wang wrote a long article criticizing the Three-Self Patriotic Movement, the state-controlled church. A few months later, Wang, his wife, and eighteen church members were imprisoned, and the Christian Tabernacle was closed. After a brief period of freedom, Wang was rearrested in 1957 and spent the next twenty-three years as a prisoner of the communist government, often kept in solitary confinement. Though a prolific writer, he was deprived of pen and paper. An accomplished pastor, he had no Bible from which to read or prepare sermons. This gifted evangelist had little contact with anyone, including his captors, and therefore no one with whom to share the faith. Wang later said, "Everything that had given me meaning as a Christian worker had been taken away from me."[1] Imagine such an existence: deprived of freedom, companionship, and the work that has defined your life. Many people facing such trials would wither in self-pity and despair.

Yet even in prison, without so much as his Bible for comfort, this seasoned leader continued to grow. Wang later said, "I had nothing to do. Nothing to do except get to know God. And for twenty years that was the greatest relationship I have ever known. But the cell was the means." Incredibly, the very thing that limited his freedom also unleashed further growth. The suffering that might have produced despair instead set Wang on the path for the greatest season of progress in his life. His advice for other believers is simple: "I was pushed into a cell, but you will have to push yourself into one. You have no time to know God. You need to build yourself a cell so you can do for yourself what persecution did for me—simplify your life and know God."[2]

The life of Wang Mingdao is a perfect illustration of growth Strategy No. 5: *Learn from Pain*. Though we may wish it were not so, suffering produces growth. If you are to reach your full potential in Christ, you will experience pain. There is no other way to be fully formed in the likeness of Jesus Christ.

That thinking is counterintuitive. Most people have a well-developed pain reflex and avoid pain whenever possible. In fact, many Christians have gravitated to the ideology that God wants each of us to experience a painless life and that, if we are faithful to him, he will bless us with endless health and wealth. We live among a generation of people who do everything they can to remove any semblance of pain from their walk with God. Feeling better has become more important than finding God.

It is tempting to believe that God wants exactly what we want—our perfect health and comfort. As with most mistaken ideologies, there are a few scriptures that can be easily misinterpreted to make that notion seem biblical. But it is not. Contrary to what you might think, there is no spiritual progress without difficulty. Everyone who wants to live a godly life in Christ will suffer. In fact, that suffering will become the catalyst for the most remarkable season of growth you have ever known—if you are open to it.

Let's dig deeper into this vitally important concept by examining four key ideas.

- Pain motivates change.
- Hardship improves character.
- Suffering binds you to Christ.
- Endurance leads to victory.

When we are finished, you will have a new understanding of the role of suffering in your life, and you will be better prepared to see and respond to God's hand at work even in the most difficult circumstances. You will also have a good handful of practical steps for applying Strategy No. 5 by responding to the negative circumstances you face in a way that will lead you closer to your full potential.

PAIN MOTIVATES CHANGE

Only present discomfort can drive you to seek a better future.

Former Bears defensive lineman William "the Refrigerator" Perry was known for his infectious smile and signature gap-tooth grin. The larger-than-life nose tackle began his football career at Clemson University and went on to play ten seasons in the National Football League, earning a championship ring in Super Bowl XX. Known also for his incredible size, Perry was dubbed "the Refrigerator" by a college classmate and often joked, "Even when I was little I was big." As a sixth grader, he weighed in at two hundred pounds.[3]

This giant of a man may have been fearless on the football field, but in daily life there was something that gave William Perry the shivers—the thought of a visit to the dentist. After twenty years of avoiding dental care, Perry had lost most of his teeth—pulling some of them himself—and his mouth was plagued by infections. That was until a Chicago-area dentist offered to extract Perry's remaining teeth and place screws in his jawbone to affix implants, a service valued at over $60,000. After months of intense work, the Fridge emerged with a new smile. "It's wonderful," he said of his new chops. "It's unbelievable. And I love them." After twenty years of avoiding the dentist, suffering chronic infections, and living with nearly constant mouth pain, what finally drove William Perry to accept the offer of dental reconstruction? It's simple. He said, "I got tired of my mouth hurting all the time."[4]

Perry's experience shows the power of Strategy No. 5: Learn from Pain. You will not seek a better future until the pain of the present becomes too great. Pain is the greatest motivator of change known to humankind. It has far more potential to drive you in the right direction than any other emotion or experience, including desire. C. S. Lewis put it this way, "We can ignore even pleasure. But pain insists upon being attended to. God whispers to us in our pleasures, speaks in our conscience, but shouts in our pains: it is His megaphone to rouse a deaf world."[5]

Someone has observed that a cat that sits on a hot stove won't do so again. That's true. Pain is a great motivator. Physical pain drives us to a physician to seek treatment. Hunger drives us to seek the nourishment we need to grow strong. Financial pain forces us to deal with debt and drives us to earn and save money. The spiritual pain of guilt, shame, and conviction brought by the Holy Spirit are what lead us to listen to the voice of God and accept his offer of salvation. We would make very little progress in this world or in our lives if we never felt discomfort.

What is your current pain point? Where are you suffering or experiencing discomfort? Is it in your relationship with God? A relationship with others? Perhaps wrongdoing or injustice by some other person? You may be dealing with the self-inflicted pain of poor life choices. Now here is the deeper question: How can you learn, change, or grow as a result of what you are suffering? How can your life be different—even better—tomorrow as a result of your response to your painful circumstances today? You can grow through pain if you will allow what you experience to drive you to self-examination and change. This is just one way that suffering produces growth.

HARDSHIP IMPROVES CHARACTER

You learn best when you suffer most.

A second aspect of learning from pain is the basic truth that hardship improves character. In other words, you learn best when you suffer most. God, at times, allows us to go through pain in order to test and refine our faith. Often, we can see that only in retrospect as we grasp the larger picture of what God has done in and through our difficulties. This is a second way in which suffering produces growth.

Many people are uncomfortable with the idea that God allows and even uses suffering to help us grow, but that truth is undeniably taught in the pages of Scripture. James stated this most clearly, saying, "Consider it pure joy, my brothers and sisters, whenever you face trials of many kinds, because you know that the testing of your faith produces perseverance. Let perseverance finish its work so that you may be mature and complete, not lacking anything" (James 1:2–4 NIV). And the writer of Hebrews was equally candid on this point: "Now no chastening for the present seemeth to be joyous, but grievous: nevertheless afterward it yieldeth the peaceable fruit of righteousness unto them which are exercised thereby" (Heb. 12:11). The word *chastening* in this verse is derived from the Greek word *paideia*, which means training. Just as athletes must exercise in training for a contest, chastisement is the necessary exercise to give experience, and make the spiritual combatant victorious. As is so often said, no pain, no gain. We cannot expect to grow stronger unless our limits are tested, and that is often a painful experience.

So why, exactly, does God allow this? What's the point? Here again the writer of Hebrews is instructive: "For whom the Lord loveth he chasteneth, and scourgeth every son whom he receiveth. If ye endure chastening, God dealeth with you as with sons; for what son is he whom the father chasteneth not?" (Heb. 12:6–7). God disciplines us because he loves us. Just as any loving parent will correct the behavior of his children, even though that may be unpleasant at the time, so God corrects us when we need it. And though that discipline may be painful, it is evidence that God cares enough about us to rectify our thoughts and actions so we can grow.

The writer of Hebrews makes a further point about the value of pain with this statement about Jesus' life and ministry. He says that Jesus, "who in the days of his flesh, when he had offered up prayers and supplications with strong crying and tears unto him that was able to save him from death, and was heard in that he feared; Though he were a Son, yet learned he obedience by the things which he suffered" (Heb. 5:7–8). If Jesus, the Son of God, had to suffer in order to become perfect, meaning complete and not lacking any human experience, and if he learned from that suffering, how much more will we grow through the trials we face?

We grow through hardship. This is the testimony of countless Christians over the centuries. Malcolm Muggeridge, the Christian journalist whom we met previously, put a contemporary voice to this experience. He wrote:

> *Contrary to what might be expected, I look back*
> *on experiences that at the time seemed especially*

> *desolating and painful with particular satisfaction. Indeed, I can say with complete truthfulness that everything I have learned in my seventy-five years in this world, everything that has truly enhanced and enlightened my existence, has been through affliction and not through happiness, whether pursued or attained. In other words, if it ever were to be possible to eliminate affliction from our earthly existence by means of some drug or other medical mumbo jumbo . . . the result would not be to make life delectable, but to make it too banal or trivial to be endurable. This, of course is what the Cross signifies. And it is the Cross, more than anything else, that has called me inexorably to Christ.[6]*

What are you suffering right now? Where is the source of pain or difficulty in your life? Rather than simply endure it as "something to get through" or worse, a meaningless chapter of your life, try reframing how you think about this circumstance. You can do that by changing the basic question you ask about your suffering. Generally, we ask *why* meaning, "Why did this happen *to me?*" That question may be legitimate, but it may be unanswerable from your current point of view. You may need the perspective of time—or even eternity—to comprehend the answer.

Also, the why question contains both a veiled accusation against God and a hidden message about yourself. The question presumes that God should not have allowed this circumstance in your life and that you are helpless to do anything about it. Those unstated assumptions trap you in a mind-set of doubt and discouragement. What if you were to reframe your thinking by asking a different question? Rather than asking *why*, try asking *what*. What can I learn from this experience? What does God have in store for me in the future? What does this difficulty make possible in my life? What can I do to grow through this? When you begin to ask a better question, you will find that God can and does use *everything* in your life to root out selfishness, develop holiness, and lead you closer to your full potential.

SUFFERING BINDS YOU TO CHRIST

You will meet Jesus in your sorrow.

A third way suffering produces growth is that it brings you closer to Jesus. You will meet Jesus in your sorrow and, like the Chinese pastor Wang Mingdao, find that your relationship with him has become deeper than ever before. This is the most precious but least expected aspect of Strategy No. 5. Your suffering will strengthen your relationship with Christ.

Jesus suffered a great deal during his earthly life and ministry. The prophet Isaiah goes so far as to describe Christ as "a man of sorrows, and acquainted with grief" (Isaiah 53:3). This poignant description of our Lord reminds us that suffering is a central aspect of his life. Jesus came to suffer and die, so when we suffer, we identify more closely with him. The apostle Paul, so finely attuned to the value of learning through painful experiences, expresses this thought beautifully: "I want to know Christ—yes, to know the power of his resurrection and participation in his sufferings, becoming like him in his death, and so, somehow, attaining to the resurrection from the dead" (Phil 3:10–11 NIV). When we suffer, we come to know Jesus in a deeper, more meaningful way, and we find him present in our suffering. We are not alone in what we endure because we know that he, too, suffered and is able to comfort us through the Holy Ghost. Jesus said, "And I will pray the Father, and he shall give you another Comforter, that he may abide with you for ever" (John 14:16). We have the presence of God with us wherever we are, even in hard places, through his Spirit.

What are you enduring now that might cause you to despair, or give up, or conclude that you cannot persevere on your journey? Are you aware that Jesus is with you right now? Do you take advantage of your ability to pray in the Holy Ghost, gaining comfort and strength for your trials? Seek the fellowship of Christ through prayer and Scripture. He will guide you to grow through—not merely in spite of—your current circumstances.

ENDURANCE LEADS TO VICTORY

The path to blessing leads through suffering.

A fourth way suffering produces growth is that when you endure, you become victorious. The path to blessing leads through suffering. This aspect of Strategy No. 5 is crucial. When you experience difficulty on your journey, you must remember that victory comes to those who persevere. No trial lasts forever, but it will produce a harvest of holiness in your life if you remain faithful.

God, at times, allows us to go through pain in order to experience the blessing that he has for us and for those we can influence with our lives. Often, our pain also serves to bring blessing to others. Until we see the big picture—what God is doing in and through the difficulties in our lives—we miss the fact that God is using it for his ultimate glory. Don't misinterpret your pain, struggles, or circumstances as either a curse from God or a roadblock that cannot be overcome. God is not punishing you; rather, he is positioning you for his purpose. Remember, "all things work together for good to them that love God, to them who are the called according to his purpose" (Rom. 8:28).

We often have the mistaken idea that suffering is something out of the ordinary for a Christian. That thinking produces arrogance in those who do not currently experience hardship, and it can produce despair in those who do. But the apostle Peter reminds us, "Beloved, think it not strange concerning the fiery trial which is to try you, as though some strange thing happened unto you: But rejoice, inasmuch as ye are partakers of Christ's sufferings; that, when his glory shall be revealed, ye may be glad also with exceeding joy" (1 Pet. 4:12–13). Once again we see that God is not surprised by our trails; he is right there in the midst of them. And what we experience will result in great blessing to ourselves and others—if not now, then certainly in the future when Jesus returns in his glory. We grow strong in the faith by learning to persevere during trying times, knowing that something greater lies on the other side of them. Remember, too, it was only after Jesus had suffered that he "became the source of eternal salvation for all who obey him" (Heb. 5:9 NIV). We must endure in order to achieve.

Perseverance is essential to growth, but it is not easy. When you are ill, facing stress at work, dealing with difficult personal relationships—or worse, persecuted for the faith as believers in some parts of the world are right now—it is challenging to keep a hopeful attitude. It helps to take the longer view on your life and circumstances. Do not be discouraged by present circumstances but keep your eyes on the bigger picture of what God is doing, not just in your life but also in the world. The apostle Paul suffered greatly in his life and ministry, yet he was able to keep this hopeful outlook. He wrote, "But we have this treasure in earthen vessels, that the excellency of the power may be of God, and not of us. We are troubled on every side, yet not distressed; we are perplexed, but not in despair; Persecuted, but not forsaken; cast down, but not destroyed; Always bearing about in the body the dying of the Lord Jesus, that the life also of Jesus might be made manifest in our body. For we which live are always delivered unto death for Jesus' sake, that the life also of Jesus might be made manifest in our mortal flesh" (2 Corinthians 4:7–11). Imagine this: your perseverance through trials actually brings glory to God by revealing his strength in you! The hardship you endure, the pain and suffering that may be your lot right now, could bring hope and strength to others as they come to realize that your endurance can come only by the grace of God. This knowledge is what allowed Paul to say, "For I reckon that the sufferings of this present time are not worthy to be compared with the glory which shall be revealed in us" (Rom. 8:18).

When I think of learning from pain, my mind invariably goes to the life of Joseph, that great patriarch who suffered so unjustly at the hands of others. He dealt with the harsh reality of rejection and hatred from his own family when his brothers sold him as a slave—only after abandoning a plot to take his life. He was taken as a captive to Egypt, where he was sold again. Just when it seemed that his life had taken a turn for the better, Joseph was thrown into prison, falsely accused of attempted rape. He languished there for years, forgotten even by his few friends. Yet through all of

Joseph's pain, God had not forgotten nor abandoned him. To the contrary, God had placed Joseph in the exact position where he could do the most good. Bible teacher John MacArthur explains it this way:

> The big picture that Joseph saw was the reality that though [his brothers] had mistreated him, it was in the purpose of God. And that purpose was so vast, and so all encompassing, and so far-reaching as really to be staggeringly amazing. Bottom line, the Lord used Joseph's suffering and his subsequent circumstances to accomplish his own sovereign purposes . . . God had a plan for the world, and in order to fulfill that plan for the world, he had a plan for the nation Israel. And in order to fulfill the plan for the nation Israel, he had a plan for Joseph. And it all was tied together.[7]

In the end Joseph related this principle to his brothers, saying, "But as for you, ye thought evil against me; but God meant it unto good, to bring to pass, as it is this day, to save much people alive" (Gen. 50:20).

You may not be able to discern the big picture right now. That's understandable. Yet it is important for you and for those whom you influence to continue trusting God, believing that his purpose is still active in your life. God has called you for a purpose. You have the potential to grow beyond where you are regardless of your current circumstances. God is sovereign, and he will not abandon you. Keep the faith. For as Paul says, "If we suffer, we shall also reign with him" (2 Tim. 2:12).

Suffering produces growth. How does that come about? The very pain that you seek to avoid will motivate change in your life. The hardships you endure become the tools that God uses to improve your character. When you suffer, you are bound ever more closely to Christ, strengthening and deepening your relationship with him. And it is your endurance through these hardships that will lead to your ultimate victory. Are you enduring some painful trial right now? Thank God for his constant presence and faithful work in your life, and keep growing.

GROWTH ACTIVITIES

It can be difficult to apply Strategy No. 5 for two reasons. The first is that we naturally resist the idea that pain can serve a positive purpose in our lives. So while we do not seek difficult circumstances, we must at least recognize that they help us to reach our full potential if we handle them well. The second reason it is difficult to apply this strategy is that we are naturally bent to be proactive and seek immediate solutions, but the lessons from suffering are often revealed gradually over time. This strategy requires patience and perseverance, which do not come easily.

Here are three growth activities for applying Strategy No. 5 in your life. Each one calls for thoughtful reflection, and none offers an easy solution to the problems you face. However, as you practice them over time, you will see the fruit of growth in your life.

REVIEW YOUR TIMELINE

In Strategy No. 3 we introduced the idea of creating a timeline of your life as a tool for seeing God at work and identifying your purpose. Use that same timeline (or create another) to review the growth you have experienced through hardship. Draw a horizontal line on a sheet of paper, representing your life from birth to the present. On that line, make a mark for each significant life event and label it. Especially note the difficult times you've faced. Label those events with a single word, such as illness, grief, or divorce. Now write one sentence that summarizes what you learned through each experience. You could write about how your faith grew, or the blessing you experienced on the other side of that hardship. Finally, connect those dots by writing a one-paragraph description of how pain has produced growth in your life. Share your findings with your growth team. This will both strengthen your conviction that God is sovereign in your life and encourage your team members who may be struggling with doubt or despair.

REFRAME YOUR LIFE

Each of us has an unseen *frame* through which we view our lives. This frame is like the lens on a pair of eyeglasses. It shapes everything you see. For example, some people see the world through the frame of victimhood. To them, every difficulty or challenge they experience is viewed as further evidence of the fact that other people control what happens to them and that they are powerless to shape their own lives. Others see the world through the frame of need. Their view of their home, income, and possessions is filtered through the idea that they do not have enough and need something more in order to be happy. There are many other negative frames, such as fear, failure, and rejection. Having a negative frame for your life is like having a pair of eyeglasses with the wrong prescription. It distorts everything you see, virtually ensuring that you will not learn from the pain you experience because the difficulties and challenges you face will only reinforce your negative view of God, yourself, and the world.

To benefit from your suffering, regardless of whether it is great or small, you will need to reframe your life in positive terms. This is like getting the correct prescription for your glasses: it puts everything into the correct focus. To reframe your thinking, first identify the major frame (or guiding idea) of your life. Is it positive or negative? (Your timeline review will be a great help in doing this.) Next, write some positive, biblical frames through which you might view yourself and your circumstances. Here are a few examples:

- *Abundance*   God has promised to supply all my needs according to his riches.
- *Holiness*   He who began a good work in me will be faithful to complete it.
- *Victory*   I am more than an overcomer through the grace of Christ my Lord.
- *Acceptance*   I am no longer a stranger to God but a closer friend.
- *Hope*   I know that in all things God works for my good because I love him and am set apart for his purpose.

Finally, restate your view of your life and circumstances through the positive frame that you have chosen. What does illness look like to a person who believes in God's ultimate healing power? How would you respond to financial pressure if you were able to see the world through the lens of God's abundance? Reframing your life and your circumstances in positive ways will ensure that you grow through your circumstances rather than being beaten down by them.

LEARN FROM THE PAST

We are not the first generation of Christians to deal with suffering. The history of God's people is one of hardship, including homelessness, hunger, injustice, and persecution. Through the centuries, many saints have been sustained and strengthened by God's grace given at just the right time. Though they suffered great hardships, they remained faithful. Hebrews 11 reminds us of the many biblical heroes who persevered through suffering. Read their stories to remind yourself of God's faithfulness. There are many historical and contemporary examples of perseverance as well. Learn from these saints by reading their writings or biographies. For example, John Wesley was ridiculed and even stoned for preaching holiness during the eighteenth century. When Wesley died on March 2, 1791, at the age of eighty-seven and surrounded by friends, he gave this marvelous testimony with his last words, "The best of all is, God is with us."[8]

Corrie ten Boom, along with her father and other family members, helped many Jews escape the Nazi Holocaust during World War II. She was imprisoned for her actions in the infamous Ravensbrück concentration camp, where she and her sister, Betsie, endured terrible suffering. Corrie later wrote about her trials in the book *The Hiding Place*. She recalled one day in the camp, just before Betsie passed away, when she had been taken to the camp infirmary. Weak from her illness, lying on a stretcher on the floor, Betsie tried to speak but was scarcely able. Corrie leaned down and was barely able to make out the dying woman's words. She said, ". . . must tell people what we have learned here. There is no pit so deep that He [God] is not deeper still."[9]

D. L. Welch, founding pastor of the church I now serve as senior pastor, was scorned by his family when he was converted in 1924. He and wife, Lottie, suffered the loss of a three-year-old child and suffered many trials and persecutions as they traveled across the South, preaching tent revivals and starting congregations before settling in Pensacola in 1933. Because of his dedication and perseverance, a great congregation stands today. Choose mentors in the faith who have weathered the storm of suffering and can testify to God's sovereignty and goodness. Immerse yourself in the lives of these saints and let their stories encourage and inspire you while you walk the difficult and painful road of suffering.

Strategy No. 5 is difficult to apply. Yet you will have to learn from pain on your journey to full potential. In the end, this strategy may also be the most rewarding. As you begin to view your life through the lens of God's redemptive work rather than focusing only on your own circumstances, you will discover a deeper kinship with Christ and spiritual resources that you were previously unaware of. I believe in you. You have the potential to rise far above the painful circumstances that you now face—or may face in the future—and become a shining example of what God can accomplish through a willing servant. Keep the faith and grow through your trials. Suffering produces growth, and I know that will be true in your life too.

ACTION LIST

1. Choose one or more growth activities from this chapter and set a time to accomplish them.

2. If you are currently facing a trial, journal about that experience and how you are growing through it.

3. If you are not currently facing a trial, reach out to someone who is. Listen and offer encouragement from scriptures such as Romans 8, 1 Corinthians 4, and Hebrews 4.

4. Conduct a self-inventory to identify lessons you have previously learned—or failed to learn—from the challenges in your life. Choose one lesson to apply to your current circumstances.

5. Share Strategy No. 5: Learn from Pain with one person today.

STRATEGY NO. 6
Practice Strategic Thinking
You Cannot Succeed Without a Plan

> *And of the children of Issachar, which were men that had understanding of the times, to know what Israel ought to do; the heads of them were two hundred; and all their brethren were at their commandment.*
> —*1 Chronicles 12:32*

Operation Overlord, the top-secret plan by Allied forces to invade France, was the turning point in World War II. On D-Day, June 6, 1944, 24,000 paratroopers landed in northern France and more than 160,000 American, British, and Canadian troops landed along a fifty-mile stretch of the Normandy coast. The operation included more than 5,000 ships and 13,000 aircraft, and by sunset the Allies had gained a foothold on the European continent, allowing more than 100,000 troops to begin the journey toward Berlin that would culminate with the unconditional surrender of the German Third Reich eleven months and one day later.

However, the now legendary D-Day invasion almost didn't take place. The fact that it did happen—and that it was successful—is testament to a crucial aspect of any major undertaking, including your growth toward full potential. Both depend on Strategy No. 6: *Practice Strategic Thinking.* Simply put, *you cannot succeed without a plan.*

During 1942 and into 1943, the advance of Adolph Hitler's Nazi regime had begun to stall. On January 14–24, 1943, President Franklin D. Roosevelt and British Prime Minister Winston Churchill met in the city of Casablanca, Morocco, to finalize Allied plans for the defeat of the Axis powers. Soviet Premier Joseph Stalin was unable to attend because the Soviets were conducting a major offensive against the German army at that time. Roosevelt and Churchill agreed that the war could end only after the unconditional surrender of Axis forces and not through a negotiated peace settlement. However, there was ongoing disagreement on *how* to bring about that surrender. Americans favored a direct assault on Germany through an invasion of France. Others argued for continuing to chip away at the German forces on the periphery of their empire. The question was not settled for five more months until American and British leaders agreed to a joint invasion of France to be conducted in 1944. That strategic decision was the first step in the joint effort that brought eventual victory, but a momentous issue remained unsettled. How could such an invasion be accomplished?

This was no small question; military leaders were planning the largest amphibious assault in history, and there were formidable obstacles. The Nazi forces had heavily fortified the French coastline and had reserve forces ready to reinforce at a moment's notice. If the Germans received even a hint of the intended Allied landing point, the invasion would certainly fail. Even without a warning, the German reserve forces could easily be mobilized to smash invading troops before they advanced beyond a beachhead. Clearly, the Allies needed an airtight strategy for the plan to succeed.

In response to this challenge, Allied forces under the direction of the London Controlling Section, a secret division of the British government, launched Operation Bodyguard. The aim of this operation was to mislead the German high command about the true intention of the Allies. The goal was to make the German leaders think the invasion of Europe would come up to a year later than the actual D-Day and would take place in either the Balkans, southern France, or Norway. Using double agents, fake radio traffic, and visual deceptions, the Allies created two fake armies, leading the Germans to believe that a great number of troops were being held in reserve for a later attack. The plan worked, and the Normandy invasion took the Germans by surprise. In fact, the deceptions were so successful that Hitler delayed sending reinforcements for more than six weeks, believing that the Normandy landing was merely a diversion. Though Allied casualties on D-Day were high—some 10,000 total with 4,414 confirmed dead—the results would have been far worse without the careful forethought that went into both Operation Overlord and Operation Bodyguard. Strategic thinking by the Allied leaders won the battle before a single soldier stepped foot on the beach.

Without a clear agreement on the outcome—the unconditional surrender of Nazi forces brought about by an invasion of Europe—World War II could have dragged on for years longer. Without a strategic plan for the invasion, the entire war could have been lost. You cannot succeed without a plan.

The same is true for you in your quest to reach your full potential. Knowing your life's purpose and having a clear vision for what you hope to accomplish are important starting points for your journey. But they will remain nothing more than a wish until backed by a solid, workable strategic plan to make them reality.

This advice is sometimes taken as unspiritual or even worldly by Christians who are concerned about the use of secular means to accomplish godly purposes. Believing that spiritual resolve and spiritual disciplines are the only tools needed to advance the Kingdom, they eschew any tactics that smack of business management or secular leadership. However, there are many good reasons why strategic thinking should be part of your plan for growth.

GOD IS A STRATEGIC THINKER

First, God is a strategic thinker. We often speak in glowing terms of God's plan for the world; however, many leaders behave as if God's plan were not really a plan at all but merely an intention. Recognizing God's supernatural ability to create reality through a mere word, they believe that God intends simply to will the salvation and sanctification of souls. But God has always operated from an overarching strategic plan. He chose Abraham to become the father of many nations so that all peoples of the world would be blessed through him. God later formed the people of Israel into a nation, his chosen people through whom the Messiah would come. God had a redemptive plan from the beginning—that he would come in flesh to die for our sins. God sent his Spirit into the lives of believers to transform them into the body of Christ and to pray for miracles and healing. God's plan continues to unfold through the church to this very day. Jesus himself had a plan for ministry. He chose twelve of his followers and designated them as apostles. After teaching them continuously for some three years, he entrusted them with his plan to teach, baptize, and make disciples.

Notice how Jesus married spiritual power with practical action in his commissioning of the disciples in Acts 1:8. He said, "But ye shall receive power, after that the Holy Ghost is come upon you: and ye shall be witnesses unto me both in Jerusalem, and in all Judæa, and in Samaria, and unto the uttermost part of the earth." The Holy Ghost would provide the power, but the disciples would undertake their mission in a strategic fashion, beginning in the holy city of Jerusalem and radiating outward in increasingly wide concentric circles. That's a strategic plan, and it was coupled with spiritual power.

We do well to recognize that prayer is our default starting point for any spiritual endeavor; however, we must also engage in critical thinking, planning, and action to accomplish our goals. After all, God does.

STRATEGY TRUMPS VISION

A second reason to engage in strategic thinking is that *how* you go about an endeavor has the power to make or break *what* you hope to do. Good intentions are worthless in the absence of a practical strategy. And strategy ultimately determines outcome. How you choose to accomplish your goal—and not the goal itself—will determine whether you are successful. Just as you cannot drive from New York to London, you cannot achieve your full potential through a regimen of complaining, isolation, procrastination, and ignorance. The things you do determine what you accomplish. Your pathway determines your destination.

Strategy trumps vision every time. To succeed in growing to your full potential, you must have a strategic plan for doing so.

FAILING TO PLAN IS PLANNING TO FAIL

A third reason you must engage in strategic thinking is that without a plan you place yourself at the mercy of chance and, perhaps worse, the intentions of other people. If you do not plan your time, others will plan it for you. Church members, clients, coworkers, and even family members all have ideas for how you should use your time and energy, or at the very least would like to involve you in what they are trying to accomplish. Without a clear plan of your own, you will default to their plans for your life—which seldom include your growth! By thinking strategically about how to reach your goals and accomplish your purpose, you guard yourself against inaction, aimlessness, and being drawn into the strategic plans of others. Their plans may be well and good, but they are not likely to move you toward your full potential. To do that, you must have a plan of your own.

Tell me your strategy for growth, and I will immediately tell you how successful you will be. Failure is sometimes dependent on circumstances beyond our control, but more often it is the strategies and the systems built to support them that determines success. Let's explore the practice of strategic thinking by examining five steps to developing a strategic plan. They are:

1. Define your goal.
2. Set your priorities.
3. Organize your time and energy.
4. Determine your method of measurement.
5. Remember the power of words.

When we are finished, you will have a clear roadmap for creating your own strategic plan for growth, and a list of practical action steps to get you started on that process. Within a short time from now, you will be able to leverage Strategy No. 6 as you begin to think strategically in your quest to reach your full potential.

STEP 1: DEFINE YOUR GOAL

You must have a destination in mind.

The first step in strategic thinking is to define your goal. To arrive at your full potential, you must have a destination in mind. Motivational speaker Zig Ziglar was fond of saying that if you aim at nothing, you will hit it every time, and that's absolutely true. And I can tell you this: if you don't know where you are going, no one else will either. It is a bit like the exchange between Alice and the Cheshire Cat in Lewis Carroll's classic book *Alice's Adventures in Wonderland*. Alice begins by asking:

> "Would you tell me, please, which way I ought to walk from here?"
>
> "That depends a good deal on where you want to get to," said the Cat.
>
> "I don't much care where—" said Alice.
>
> "Then it doesn't matter which way you walk," said the Cat.[1]

Until you know precisely what you hope to accomplish, there is no point in defining your strategy. You must choose a destination before you can determine which actions steps will get you there. Remember that strategy trumps vision, so the plan you make will take you to a specific destination—whether it's the one you want or not. That means it is vital that you first see the big picture and clearly define the outcome you want to achieve. If you don't, your action plan could take you to the wrong destination. As futurist Alvin Toffler put it, "You've got to think about 'big things' while you're doing small things, so that all the small things go in the right direction."[2]

What is your growth goal? We have already discussed the importance of knowing your purpose in Strategy No. 1, so you have likely given some thought to this. Your growth goal, however, is more specific than your purpose. Your purpose states what you are doing from the 30,000-foot level. It is the broadest possible look at your life. Your growth goal will bring that purpose into closer view by making it more specific. For example, your purpose may be to proclaim the gospel of Jesus Christ to the world. That's a macro statement of what your life is about. However, it is not a goal because it lacks a few important characteristics. A good goal defines your purpose more narrowly. Here are a few example goals related to the purpose of proclaiming the gospel to the world:

- To present the gospel to thirty unchurched people in my county this month.
- To baptize fifteen new converts this year.
- To be ordained in my denomination within the next five years.

Notice a few things each of these goals shares. Each one is *specific, measurable, actionable, realistic,* and *time bound.* In other words, they are *S.M.A.R.T.* goals. Once you have discovered your purpose, you can formulate a goal or goals, which are specific achievements that make your purpose take shape in real life.

What is your purpose? What S.M.A.R.T. goal would help that purpose become reality in your life? Perhaps you have more than one goal. I recommend adopting a maximum of three to five goals in any one season of life because you can realistically concentrate on only a few things at a time. You may need to prioritize your goals because some may be prerequisites for others. For example, you may need to complete your education or acquire specialized training before achieving the larger goals that support your purpose.

To think strategically, you must begin with the end in mind, as Steven Covey puts it.[3] First, identify your purpose. Everything flows from that. Next, choose a select few goals that, if achieved, will make that purpose take shape in your life. This is the first step in creating a strategic plan.

STEP 2: SET YOUR PRIORITIES

Choose what you won't do.

The second step in strategic thinking is to set your priorities. Another way to understand this is choosing what you *won't* do. There are two important aspects to this. The first deals with *what* you do, and the second concerns *how* you do it. Let's talk first about the importance of determining what you will and will not do.

Many of us who are called to ministry are very good at saying "yes." We have said yes to the call of God for salvation, and we said yes to Christ's call to ministry. We want to reach people for Christ, and that often means being available to them with our time and attention. We want to achieve our purpose and accomplish our goals, and it can be tempting to say yes to every opportunity that comes our way. This is also true in the business world. If you want to advance your career, grow a business, or reach your full potential, you will have to get good at saying no.

In reality, saying yes to one thing always means saying no to something else because you have only so much time, energy, and money. So if you say yes to a new car, you may be saying no to new carpet or a summer vacation. If you say yes to a speaking engagement, you say no to several hours of family time that you might have otherwise enjoyed. If you say yes to watching television, you are saying no to reading. Setting priorities is choosing the things you will say yes to—and being clear about the things to which you'll say no.

If you cannot set your own priorities, others will set them for you. Every request you get, every phone call, every invitation, every opportunity is a priority decision. When you say yes to things that do not support your objectives, you are saying no to yourself. When you say no to requests for your time and energy that do not support your goals, you are saying yes to yourself and no to the goals and priorities of another person. Though this sounds harsh, it is a necessary part of having a balanced life that places your health, your family, and your spiritual life first so that you can reach your potential. Otherwise, you will wind up feeling tired, stressed, and frustrated, and you will not achieve your full potential.

If you are to accomplish your goals, what activities will you need to say yes to? What things will you simply not have time for, even if they seem like good opportunities? List the strategic actions that will further your progress, and, just as important, list the things that will not move you toward that goal.

A second aspect of setting priorities is to determine *how* you will accomplish your objectives—the behaviors, attitudes, and tactics you will employ. Another word for these kinds of priorities is *values*. Your values set the parameters on your methods and behavior. These priorities are like the safety features on a highway: they're intended to keep you between the white lines and headed in the right direction. First, there are the lines themselves, the reflective strips along the road that define the edges. Without them, you could easily veer into oncoming traffic or stray into a ditch. The lines limit the path you may travel, but that's really a good thing. Outside the lines on many roadways there is a rumble strip, indentations in the pavement that produce a loud rumbling sound when driven over. If you are distracted and stray over the line, the rumble strip should get your attention. If it doesn't, there are guardrails that should keep you from plunging over embankments.

Your priorities function like these highway features by limiting the path of your travel to keep you from going astray in your pursuit of a goal. For example, if honesty is one of your priorities, you won't be deceptive or even shade the truth in order to advance yourself. That means you might miss some opportunities that could have come your way had you been willing to compromise, but you won't stray into unethical territory. If you place a priority on teamwork or inclusion, you will work collaboratively and value the input of others. That could slow down your decision making or your creative process, but it will guard you against becoming arrogant or dictatorial in your leadership style.

How do you want to go about your pursuit of full potential? What are the "ditches" that you want to avoid on your journey? What will be your highest values? These priorities will mean saying no to some behaviors or tactics but saying yes to your highest internal values. Determining these priorities is the second step in creating your strategic plan.

STEP 3: ORGANIZE YOUR TIME AND ENERGY

Make the most of your most important resource: yourself.

The third step in strategic thinking is to organize your time and energy. If you are to achieve your full potential you must learn to make the most of your most precious but limited resource—yourself. While this may sound like simple time management, the issue of self-management is much more complex.

Time management is about exercising control over the amount of time spent on specific activities, especially to increase efficiency or productivity. Over the years, a number of time management theorists have developed systems for allocating and tracking the use of time, especially time spent on work. You may now be using a time management system, which usually includes a calendar and a task list. Such tools are helpful in organizing daily tasks in keeping with your priorities, but they are not a total solution for managing your time and energy. Perhaps you have already discovered that a well-planned day may look good on paper, but implementing it in the real world is not as easy as it seems. If you are running late in the morning, constantly interrupted by phone calls or text messages, hustling to get home for dinnertime, and too tired in the evening to interact with family, the carefully crafted plan will amount to nothing. To reach your full potential, you will have to go beyond prioritizing tasks and manage these two crucial elements of your life: your *energy* and your *interruptions*.

Your ability to function at a high level depends on being alert, focused, and energetic. You can accomplish more in a short time when you are at full energy than in hours of labor when you are tired, stressed, or hungry. To reach your full potential, you must be spiritually, physically, and mentally alert and engaged.

The problem for many of us is that we try to do too much. Wrongly believing that we can burn the candle at both ends, we cram too much activity into each day. As a result, we are tempted to skip a balanced meal in favor of junk food, stay up too late to "catch up," and blow off our exercise and devotional routines. As a result, we are tired, lethargic, and not able to concentrate long enough to be productive. To manage your energy, here are four things you should do consistently.

1. Establish a bedtime and a morning routine. Your day starts around 10:00 p.m. when you determine how much rest you will have for the following morning. It continues at your rising time, when you decide whether you will enter the day spiritually refreshed and properly fueled or stressed and hungry. Create bedtime and morning routines that care for your spiritual and physical needs and provide a consistent sleep pattern. Most people get too little sleep. The average person sleeps less than 7.5 hours per night, though most need at least eight and some as much as nine hours.[4]

2. Eat and exercise properly. Nutrition and fitness have a tremendous impact on your energy level and overall feeling of vitality. When you are properly fueled, you will feel better and be more alert. Exercise also affects your overall energy level. Though it may seem counterintuitive, you will likely be *more* energetic after exercising than before. Pay close attention to your eating and exercise habits, and make adjustments as needed.

3. Budget your energy, not just your time. You probably already know the time of the day when your energy and alertness are at their peak. For many people, that is first thing in the morning. These "morning people" are insufferable to "night owls," who seem to come alive when the sun goes down. You will be far more effective if you schedule your most important tasks at the times when your energy is at its peak. That could mean ensuring that you have time to accomplish your major task for the day before 9:00 a.m. For some, it might mean putting off the tasks that require most concentration until later in the day. Adopt a daily rhythm that fits your energy patterns, regardless of what others see as "normal."

4. Schedule your interruptions. Interruptions are the point at which other people's priorities invade your schedule. That could come in the form of a text message or phone call, an emergency, a request for information, or a drop-in visitor. The flow of interruptions has escalated considerably in recent years as virtually anyone in the world can have access to you at any moment through electronic communications. Managing your own time and energy means placing some limits on the ability of others to interrupt you. Though it may sound contradictory, you can manage your own time best by scheduling interruptions. Here are some ways to do that.

- *Work from home.* When possible, avoid the interruptions that accompany office life by working from home.
- *Go offline.* Shut down electronic interruptions by going offline. Shut off notifications from your email and social

media accounts. Turn off your phone and disconnect from Wi-Fi. Create an electronic bubble for yourself so that you can concentrate during times of peak energy.

- *Group appointments.* Many appointments are really scheduled interruptions, and you can minimize their impact by grouping them. If possible, schedule all appointments or meetings on a single day. Though that day will be action packed, it will free the remaining days for focused work.

- *Allow some flextime.* Of course, you cannot schedule or eliminate all interruptions. You can reduce their impact by ensuring that you have some flextime in your week. Avoid scheduling your time so tightly that there is no room for an unexpected opportunity or emergency.

- *Learn to say no.* Remember that you can refuse some interruptions. You do not have to take every phone call, respond to every request, attend every meeting, or accept every invitation. Having a clear set of priorities will make it easier for you to avoid some interruptions by simply saying no to them.

To enact your strategic plan, you will have to learn to organize your time and energy. Once you do, take action. A quote widely attributed to French military and political leader Napoleon Bonaparte says, "Take time to deliberate, but when the time for action comes, stop thinking and go in." To that I would add only these words: Go all in. Make the most of your most precious but limited resource, yourself.

STEP 4: DETERMINE YOUR METHOD OF MEASUREMENT

Every goal can be measured.

The fourth step in strategic thinking is to determine your method of measurement. Every goal can be measured. If not, it would be merely a wish or a dream. To determine whether or not you are successful in reaching your goal, you must define both your ultimate picture of success and the incremental steps that lead to it.

When Jesus gave his disciples direction for their ministry, he gave them a way to understand its effectiveness also. In Jesus' parable of the sower, he said this about the possible results of ministry of the Word: "And other fell on good ground, and did yield fruit that sprang up and increased; and brought forth, some thirty, and some sixty, and some an hundred" (Mark 4:8). We can measure our progress; it tells us where we have been, where we are, and where we are going.

Here are some strategic questions you must consider as you determine how to measure your progress toward full potential.

- What will it look like for me to be living at my full potential?

- What objective measures would indicate growth in that direction?

- If I had to choose only *one* measure of success, what would it be?

- Is my measure of success objective? That is, can it be stated in quantifiable terms?

- If my measure of success is subjective, who, other than I, can render a judgment about it?
- How often will I evaluate my progress?
- What form will that evaluation take?
- How will I process the results of my evaluation and incorporate them into my growth plan?

If your goals are properly stated, they will be measurable. Do not make the mistake of setting a goal and then ignoring it. Refer to your goals often and measure your progress at regular intervals. Otherwise, your strategic objectives could peter out and amount to nothing.

STEP 5: REMEMBER THE POWER OF WORDS

*The things you think and say can make
or break your strategic plan.*

The final step in strategic thinking is to remember the power of words. The things you think and say can make or break your strategic plan. To carry out your strategic plan, you must infuse positive, hopeful words into your mind, your heart, and your speech.

Many biblical passages reinforce the concept of the power of words to build up or tear down, perhaps none more dramatically than Proverbs 18:21, which reads, "Death and life are in the power of the tongue." The words you say, both to yourself and to others, really can be life affirming or life destroying. God created the world by the power of his Word, and our words have power too. You know that when you are criticized or belittled, it wounds your spirit. Likewise, when you are affirmed or complimented, you brighten inside and outside. You have experienced the power of words.

Recognize also that your internal words have power, even though not expressed aloud. The things you say to yourself about your potential, your growth, and your progress can either advance your progress or set it back. Think of the effect these words can have on your spirit, even if they remain only in your thoughts:

- "Stupid! Why did I do that?"
- "I'm not very good at this, so it probably won't work."
- "I hope I don't make a fool of myself again."
- "How come I'm not as smart (or capable or talented) as she is?"
- "I'm such a loser!"

Many people are defeated by their own words before the battle ever begins.

Now think of the affirming, empowering effect you can have on yourself through the power of good thoughts and words. How would it feel to hear these things and really believe they are true?

- "You can do this!"
- "I believe in you."
- "You are a totally new person in Christ."
- "I see great things in store for you!"

Your own words can build you up, inspire your confidence, and help you succeed in reaching your goals. And your words have power over others. The apostle Paul wrote, "Do not let any unwholesome talk come out of your mouths, but only what is helpful for building others up according to their needs, that it may benefit those who listen" (Eph. 4:29 NIV). Let your words advance you and others toward the goal of reaching your full potential. Eradicate negative talk, complaining, faultfinding, and insults from your mind and your speech. Practice the habit of affirming yourself and others to give hope for the future.

GROWTH ACTIVITIES

Sun Tzu, the military general, strategist, and philosopher of ancient China, observed this in his classic work, *The Art of War*, "When your strategy is deep and far-reaching, then what you gain by your calculations is much, so you can win before you even fight. When your strategic thinking is shallow and near-sighted, then what you gain by your calculations is little, so you lose before you do battle. Much strategy prevails over little strategy, so those who have no strategy cannot help but be defeated. Therefore it is said that victorious warriors win first and then go to war, while defeated warriors go to war first and then seek to win."[5] I couldn't agree more with the concept that to be successful, you must learn to think strategically. Show me your plan for growth, and I will tell you how successful you will be. A strong plan, well executed, will lead to a good result. Here are some practical growth activities that will assist you in creating a strategic plan for growth.

CLARIFY YOUR OBJECTIVES

Many people are able to state a goal that is specific, measurable, actionable, realistic, and time bound, but they struggle to identify the objectives that will advance them toward the goal. Too often, they become mired in activities that sound interesting but do not produce growth, or accept opportunities that advance the agenda of others more than their own growth goals. To clarify your objectives, first write your goal being sure that it is S.M.A.R.T. Next, write a brief answer to this question: "What would have to be true for that goal to become reality?" You might come up with things like these:

- I would have to complete a bachelor's degree.
- I would need to save $5,000.
- I would have to be in an accountability partnership or small group.

The items you list will be good candidates for your primary objectives. Create no more than three to five objectives per goal, and ensure that each one directly contributes to reaching the goal. These objectives will become your filter for saying yes or no to any opportunity that involves your time, energy, and resources.

Also clarify your objectives related to behavior and tactics you will use to advance your goal. Remember, another good term for these objectives is *values*. To clarify your values, complete this sentence: "I would like to be known by others as _____." List as many descriptors as you wish. You might come up with terms like these:

- Truthful
- Bold
- Visionary
- Loving
- Positive

The terms you list will be good candidates for your core values, the operating objectives that define who you are and how you go about reaching your full potential. Keep your list short enough to memorize and repeat often. Five to seven is a good number of stated values. Share the results of this exercise with your Growth Team.

AFFIRM YOURSELF AND OTHERS

Your words have the power to make or break your growth plan. If you are a person who struggles with feelings of self-doubt or a poor self-image, you can benefit from a simple exercise in affirmation. Begin by listing positive, affirming statements that will energize and empower you. You need look no further than scripture for the kinds of concepts that will build your self-concept, though you can add other statements as well. You might list statements like these:

- I am an overcomer!
- I am loved by God.
- I can do all things through Christ who gives me strength.
- I am a new creation.
- Nothing is impossible with God.

Next, choose an affirmation to meditate on each day for the coming week. You can choose a different statement for each day. Say it to yourself each morning. Repeat it several times throughout the day, and affirm it again at the close of the day. Also state this affirmation to at least one other person, substituting the words *you are* for *I*. Notice the effect this has on your mood, your energy, and your feelings about yourself and your circumstances.

LEARN FROM A MENTOR

Choose a person whom you believe is reaching their full potential and ask about their growth planning process. This could be as simple as a five-minute phone call or a more extended conversation, even a longer-term mentoring relationship. Ask questions like these to help you understand the way this mentor thinks strategically about growth:

- What is the most important factor in your personal growth?
- Do you have a purpose statement for your life? If so, can you share it?
- What are your top three goals right now?
- How do you measure progress toward your goals?
- What have you learned about using time- or task-management systems?
- How have you discerned which opportunities to say yes to and which to decline?
- What can you share about your daily and weekly routines?
- Who are some of your mentors?
- How frequently do you assess yourself and your growth?
- How frequently to you evaluate progress toward your goals?
- What is the best advice you can offer on reaching your full potential?

From your discoveries, distill three to five action items that you can implement right away. Also, share your findings with your Growth Team so they can benefit from your mentor as well.

Strategic thinking is an essential skill for every leader and everyone who wants to achieve their full potential. You cannot succeed without a plan. However, with a practical, strategic growth plan, you are certain to make progress! As you learn to translate your purpose into goals, objectives, and the daily actions that advance them, your growth will accelerate rapidly. Keep the big things in mind, and be sure that the little things all point toward them, and you will get there. I believe you can do this!

ACTION LIST

1. Choose one or more growth activities that will advance your strategic thinking and set a deadline for implementing them.

2. Conduct a checkup with your Growth Team on the Rule of Five. Share the positive effects you are seeing in your lives and encourage one another to be disciplined in this practice.

3. If you already have a growth plan in place, evaluate it with the concept of strategic thinking in mind. Ensure that your goals are S.M.A.R.T. and that you have clear objectives to support them.

4. If you do not have a growth plan in place, create one now using the five steps outlined in this chapter. Share your plan with your Growth Team and invite feedback.

5. Share Strategy No. 6: Practice Strategic Thinking with someone today.

STRATEGY NO. 7

Sacrifice Good for Best

You Must Give Up to Go Up

And yet I will show you the most excellent way.
—1 Corinthians 12:31 NIV

It was late in the evening. Darkness had descended on the city, and only moonlight illuminated their way. The parley had been fraught with tension as old comrades, veterans of the long campaign, had become wary of another. Only loyalty bound them together, and hope. They were loyal to their leader—a visionary, a prophet according to some. A terrorist, others said. Like anyone seeking a new order, he had accumulated zealous followers and enemies who were even more fanatical. There had been rumors of a coup, followed by rumors of assassination. Supporters were deserting in large numbers. Even top lieutenants mistrusted one another. Yet they remained, bound together by the hope of a new world.

For a political insurgent, no place remains safe for long, so they made their way out of the safe house and into the hill country. Who knew when the attack would come, or from where? Special forces own the night, the teacher had told them. Keep a watch. But they were not soldiers, really. Dreamers. And so they dreamed, falling into a dull sleep while their leader, alone and deeply troubled, pondered the coming storm.

"Going a little farther, he fell with his face to the ground and prayed, 'My Father, if it is possible, may this cup be taken from me. Yet not as I will, but as you will.'

"Then he returned to his disciples and found them sleeping. 'Couldn't you men keep watch with me for one hour?' he asked Peter. 'Watch and pray so that you will not fall into temptation. The spirit is willing, but the flesh is weak.'

"He went away a second time and prayed, 'My Father, if it is not possible for this cup to be taken away unless I drink it, may your will be done.'

"When he came back, he again found them sleeping, because their eyes were heavy. So he left them and went away once more and prayed the third time, saying the same thing.

"Then he returned to the disciples and said to them, 'Are you still sleeping and resting? Look, the hour has come, and the Son of Man is delivered into the hands of sinners. Rise! Let us go! Here comes my betrayer!'" (Matt. 26:39–46 NIV).

Jesus, on the last night of his earthly life, experienced and modeled what everyone who seeks something more from life must face. He demonstrated a practice I refer to as Strategy No. 7: *Sacrifice Good for Best*. I realize some may find it odd to refer to the Garden Prayer of our Lord as an illustration of a growth strategy, yet his life and ministry bear out this very idea: You must give up to go up.

Jesus gave up the splendor of heaven in order to walk among us, making himself nothing. As a result, he was exalted to the highest place (see Phil. 2:5–11). "Though he were a Son, yet learned he obedience by the things which he suffered; And being made perfect, he became the author of eternal salvation unto all them that obey him" (Heb. 5:8–9). In order to lay hold of the salvation that Jesus sought for each one of us, he had to surrender something of great value—his very life. He sacrificed something good for something even better. Jesus' last temptation, there in the garden, was the same as his first, in the wilderness: to do the Father's will without giving up the comforts of this life. Compare this passage with Jesus' temptation as recorded in Matthew 4:1–11. The common element is the appeal of gaining something greater without personal cost. In both cases, Jesus withstood this challenge. He realized that he must surrender what he had in order to become the savior. He was willing to give up to go up.

Sacrificing good for best is the most difficult of all growth strategies. Some things must be left behind in order to go further with Christ, and that is always painful. Personally, this has been my greatest challenge in growing toward my full potential. The easiest decisions I have ever made were choices between right and wrong. Though it was sometimes tempting to choose the easier, selfish way, I could easily see the difference between the two. Good and evil stand in stark contrast. The toughest choices I have faced are those between good and best. There have been times I was unable to give a reasonable explanation for the choices I've made, only that God's best demanded it. The defining moments in my life have come when I was called upon by the Lord to give up good things for the best things.

The difficulty in this is that the "good" things really are good. There is nothing wrong with comfort and security. Certainly we all long for this. There is no sin in possessing wealth or having a good job or being surrounded by friends. We all seek these things. Yet the enemy of God's perfect will is often the good things that you now enjoy because they make you complacent and comfortable, or because they insulate you from risk, or because God simply has something greater in mind for you. To achieve God's best in our lives, we must be willing to surrender anything that prevents us from taking hold of it. Everyone who reaches for the high calling of God in Christ Jesus must face this challenge. As French literary critic Charles du Bos put it, "The important thing is this: to be able at any moment to sacrifice what we are for what we could become."[1] When you are able to grasp that principle and apply it to your life, you will overcome the last barrier to reaching your full potential.

Let's apply Strategy No. 7 by examining five key areas in which you may be called upon to sacrifice good for best. Though these are not the only good things you might need to surrender, they are the most common:

- Friends
- Security
- Past Success
- Personal Ambition
- Immediate Gratification

When we are finished, you will have not only an understanding of this strategy but also a good idea of which good things may stand between you and your full potential. And you will have a clear action plan that will help you make the necessary changes to your life.

FRIENDS

You must give up the relationships that hold you back.

The first good thing that you may have to surrender in order to lay hold of God's best is a friend. You must surrender the friendships—or any relationships—that would hold you back from growing to your full potential. Though this is a hard lesson, it is vital that you allow nothing, not even your relationships with others, to stand between you and the call of God on your life.

One of the most troubling teachings of Jesus is found in Luke 14:26, where Jesus turns to a large crowd of would-be followers and delivers this sobering statement: "If any man come to me, and hate not his father, and mother, and wife, and children, and brethren, and sisters, yea, and his own life also, he cannot be my disciple." This seems confusing. The gospel of Jesus Christ is about love, not hate, so it seems harsh and unrealistic for Jesus to ask his followers to despise even their immediate family members. However, this teaching is not cruel when properly understood, and it takes us to the heart of this growth strategy.

First, it is important to understand the meaning of the word *hate* as used in this verse. We nearly always use this word to describe feelings of animosity, a strong aversion, or even a violently negative reaction to someone or something. That is not Jesus' meaning here. In teaching his followers the high cost of discipleship, Jesus conveyed in very strong terms that no person could claim a higher loyalty upon them than he did. This is a call not to loathe the good people who have loved and nurtured you throughout life. It is a warning to turn away from anything or anyone who might hold you back from full devotion to Christ. You have to give up the good for the best.

Jesus modeled this principle in his own life. On one occasion, early in Jesus' ministry when he had begun to draw large crowds and lots of controversy, his mother and brothers came to find him. They believed that he was "beside himself," meaning out of his mind, and they wanted to take him home so he wouldn't embarrass himself any further (Mark 3:21). At that moment, Jesus realized that even those he loved most did not understand what he was doing. So when someone told him that his family had arrived and wanted to see him, Jesus said, "Who is my mother, or my brethren? And he looked round about on them which sat about him, and said, Behold my mother and my brethren! For whosoever shall do the will of God, the same is my brother, and my sister, and mother" (Mark 3:33–35). Jesus was willing to sacrifice even his family relationships in order fulfill his mission. Thankfully, his mother and at least one brother, James, later came to see him as their Messiah.

I have practiced this in my life, and I can tell you that it is always difficult. There have been times when I had to let go of friendships with people who were not tuned in to the same goals and dreams I was. These were not evil people. I genuinely liked them and enjoyed their company. But they were not able to go with me on the journey God had led me to so I had to let them go. What relationships may be holding you back from growth? Do you have friends who do not believe in your dreams? Do they subtly try to dissuade you from seeking a higher calling? Do you have family members who do not understand or support your need to grow? Let me be clear: I do not advocate divorce or neglect of your dependents. However, you may need to make it clear even to those closest to you that your relationship with Christ must come first in your life. If you accept the expectations others have for you, especially negative expectations, you will never grow to your full potential. You may need to give up some relationships in order to go up.

SECURITY

*You must give up the comforts that mean
more to you than Jesus.*

A second good thing that you may have to surrender in order to lay hold of God's best is security. You must surrender the comforts that mean more to you than Jesus does. By now, the term *comfort zone* has become a bit cliché among Christians. We have all heard many times that we must get out of our comfort zone in order to follow God's leading. Yet this concept remains true even if the term is a bit over used. We all have something that gives us a sense of comfort or security. Perhaps for you that is your home, or your job, the familiarity of your daily routine, or the wealth you have accumulated. Those are good things, all of them. Yet any one of them may stand in the way of reaching your full potential to the extent that it hinders you from moving into new experiences in order to grow. When your comforts mean more to you than Christ, you must give them up in order to go up.

We see this concept clearly in the biblical story of the man who came to Jesus asking what he must do to gain eternal life (see Mark 10:17–23). After a brief exchange, Jesus seemed to realize that this man, though sincere in his desire to change, had a great attachment to wealth. Jesus cared deeply about this struggling soul, so he said to him: "One thing thou lackest: go thy way, sell whatsoever thou hast, and give to the poor, and thou shalt have treasure in heaven: and come, take up the cross, and follow me" (Mark 10:21). With that, the man went away sad, for he discovered that to follow Jesus would mean the sacrifice of his great wealth—and the comfort, power, and security that went with it.

We do not know for sure which choice that man eventually made, but we do know that giving up personal comfort is a huge challenge and often hinders growth. Likely, you have already faced this in your journey with God. To follow Christ fully, you may have realized that you would have to surrender some habits or practices that you used to draw pleasure from. Or you may have discovered that being a disciple would require the sacrifice of a portion of your income, given back to God as a tithe. Such choices are difficult to make because they zero in on the question that lies at the very heart of being a disciple: Whom do I trust more, God or me? Growing to your full potential will always involve trusting God more than self, evidenced by the willingness to step out of your comfort zone when called to do so.

That is exactly what great heroes of the faith have always done. Moses, though he was raised as a prince of Egypt, chose to surrender the comfort, power, and wealth of the royal household in order to become the deliverer of God's people (Heb. 11:24 – 27). "By faith Abraham, when he was called to go out into a place which he should after receive for an inheritance, obeyed; and he went out, not knowing whither he went. By faith he sojourned in the land of promise, as in a strange country, dwelling in tabernacles with Isaac and Jacob, the heirs with him of the same promise" (Heb. 11:8–9). Abraham was a wealthy man some seventy-five years of age when God called him. To leave his home and family at that point meant the sacrifice of his life's work. Yet he was willing to give up in order to go up.

Following Jesus may cost the dearest thing you possess. God does not deal with everyone the same way, but he does deal with each person specifically. That means the sacrifices you are called to make may be different from those around you. God will never ask you to give up what you love in order to punish you; rather, he asks you to step into something better, a higher level in life. What things mean the most to you? Your home? Your position or status in your community? Your career, wealth, or income? Your sense of security or safety? Mark these well, for they may be the very things that stand between you and your full potential. Jesus asks, "For what shall it profit a man, if he shall gain the whole world, and lose his own soul?" (Mark 8:36). How tragic it would be to hold onto the good things in life while sacrificing God's highest calling for you.

PAST SUCCESS

Give up the achievements of yesterday.

A third good thing you may need to give up in order to lay hold of God's best is past success. You must abandon the achievements of yesterday to grow into God's future. This is difficult because the successes of the past are our best evidence of God's presence and power in our lives. But the victories that God won for you last week or last year or ten years ago may be merely stepping-stones toward his ultimate goal, your full potential.

It is tempting to memorialize the success of the past. You may see this in an athlete who continues to live on the thrill of bygone victories, years after he has left the field of competition. Or you may see a retailer that continues to use an outdated business model because the leaders' thinking is stuck in past days when they were highly successful. On a personal level, it is difficult to risk the perks or prestige that have come with past achievements to begin a new venture. But that is what each of us must be willing to do in order to lay hold of the *more* that God has for us. The key is to realize that with God, the future is always better than the past—no matter how good that past may seem. Steve Maraboli, a behavioral scientist specializing in leadership dynamics, put it this way: "As I look back on my life, I realize that every time I thought I was being rejected from something good, I was actually being redirected to something better."[2] Sometimes God will ask you to let something go because he has something better in store for you.

The apostle Paul had an exemplary background in education and religion. He was brought up at the feet of Gamaliel, a renowned rabbi, and was taught to obey God's law perfectly. He was "circumcised the eighth day, of the stock of Israel, of the tribe of Benjamin, an Hebrew of the Hebrews; as touching the law, a Pharisee; Concerning zeal, persecuting the church; touching the righteousness which is in the law, blameless" (Phil. 3:5–6). At a young age, Paul had achieved great things in his career. Yet he realized that the call of God upon his life would mean the sacrifice of all that—his position, connections, opportunities, and everything else he had gained. He said, "But what things were gain to me, those I counted loss for Christ. Yea doubtless, and I count all things but loss for the excellency of the knowledge of Christ Jesus my Lord: for whom I have suffered the loss of all things, and do count them but dung, that I may win Christ" (Phil. 3:7–8). He was willing to give up in order to go up.

What are the greatest successes or achievements of your life? What can you point to as evidence that you have done something worthwhile? Perhaps it is the diploma hanging on your wall, or the awards on your mantle, or the title by which others address you. Now here's the challenge: would you scrap all of that, if necessary, and begin again in order to achieve something even better? Would you take the risk of leaving those things behind to reach out for your full potential, even though that potential is still just a dream? When you are willing to give up the success or achievements of your past, you are ready to grow into God's future.

PERSONAL AMBITION

Give up the things you desire for yourself.

A fourth good thing you may need to give up in order to lay hold of God's best is your personal ambition. You must be willing to surrender the noble dreams that you have for yourself in order to grow into what God envisions for you. This is difficult because it cuts to the core of who we are and what we long for. Often, our dreams and ambitions are good things—but they may be *our* good things and not God's. The challenge is to set aside what we want in favor of what God would have for us.

Often the next step that God has in mind for us involves the sacrifice of ourselves for others. To grow into the person God wants you to be, you will have to face choices between what you want and what others need. Smallness is putting yourself, your needs, and your desires first in every situation. Greatness is found in sacrificing yourself, and sometimes your dreams, on behalf of others. This is the life that Jesus modeled for us, and learning to live this way is a major growth point for every person.

Ironically, when we do learn to put Christ and his kingdom first, we gain far more than we lose. Jesus put it this way: "For whosoever will save his life shall lose it; but whosoever shall lose his life for my sake and the gospel's, the same shall save it" (Mark 8:35). Giving up your ambitions, needs, and wants is not a bad thing because we usually want too little for ourselves rather than too much. When we learn to seek Jesus and his kingdom, putting him and others ahead of ourselves, it opens the door to a greater way of living.

In his well-known book on business principles, *Good to Great*, author Jim Collins shows that this spiritual practice is also a highly practical way of living. In his study of companies that had gone from being merely good companies to great ones, Collins found a common denominator in the companies' leaders. Many of them displayed a paradoxical mix of intense determination and profound humility. They usually had a personal sense of investment in the company and its success, so much so that personal ego and financial rewards were less important to them than the long-term success of the team and the company. In other words, the leaders who were able to lead others from good to great were those willing to surrender their own needs or desires for the benefit of others.[3]

What are the good things that you envision for yourself? Perhaps you long for success, the acclamation of others, or financial security. Your personal ambitions may include any number of legitimate things that would benefit you. Are you willing to surrender them, if needed, to advance the cause of Christ and to meet the needs of others? When achieving something for others becomes more important than achieving something for yourself, you are ready to give up and go up.

IMMEDIATE GRATIFICATION

Give up the need for instant results.

A fifth good thing you may need to give up in order to lay hold of God's best is immediate gratification. You must be willing to surrender—or in this case, delay—the reward for your efforts in order to reach your full potential. This is difficult because we live in a culture that values progress, and we all long for immediate results. Whether it is getting in better physical condition, saving money, or completing an education, we want to see results *now*! But growth takes time and always requires effort. It does not come easily and certainly not immediately. To go further toward your full potential, you must surrender your need to see instant results for your efforts.

A quotation widely attributed to Muhammad Ali illustrates the need for patience in seeking achievement: "I hated every minute of training, but I said, 'Don't quit. Suffer now and live the rest of your life as a champion.'" Every athlete knows the truth behind that statement. You must give up a level of freedom during training and delay the hoped-for reward until the contest is completed. The apostle Paul had this in mind when he wrote, "For our light affliction, which is but for a moment, worketh for us a far more exceeding and eternal weight of glory" (2 Cor. 4:17). Isaiah, too, understood the need for patience when he prophesied about God's exiled people, "And the ransomed of the Lord shall return, and come to Zion with songs and everlasting joy upon their heads: they shall obtain joy and gladness, and sorrow and sighing shall flee away" (Isa. 35:10).

To grow to your full potential, you must think of your life as an athlete thinks about winning or an investor thinks about building wealth: it takes time. You must forego short-term rewards in order to achieve a higher purpose. To better yourself intellectually, you will have to sacrifice time that could be spent in leisure in order to study. The result will be a stronger intellect, but it will take time. To achieve more financially, you may have to make an investment of your income or your labor that will not bear fruit overnight. In time, you will see the results. How patient are you? How long are you willing to wait to see the payoff for your efforts? Novelist Robert Louis Stevenson reportedly said, "Don't judge each day by the harvest you reap but by the seeds that you plant." When you are able to sacrifice immediate gain for future growth, you are ready to give up and go up.

IT'S WORTH IT

Strategy No. 7 is incredibly difficult to apply. The good things you are already enjoying insulate you from the desire to reach for your full potential. It is easy to become complacent. And the risk of loss can be frightening. What if you don't reach the next level? What if you give up relationships and comforts and perks but the hoped-for reward never materializes? If you feel that hesitation in your walk with Jesus, you're not alone. This seventh growth strategy points to a crossroad that every follower of Jesus Christ must face. There, many hesitate, then turn away in fear. Peter, the great apostle, gave voice to this apprehension in Luke 18:28 when he said to Jesus, "Lo, we have left all and followed thee." The disciples had indeed sacrificed everything—home, family, livelihood, reputation—to follow Jesus. Was it worth it? That is the silent question behind Peter's statement.

Jesus answered that question with a resounding yes. He responded to Peter, saying, "Verily I say unto you, There is no man that hath left house, or parents, or brethren, or wife, or children, for the kingdom of God's sake, Who shall not receive manifold more in this present time, and in the world to come life everlasting" (Luke 18:29–30). With God, you always gain more than you lose. The future is always brighter than the past. Your sacrifice is always rewarded. Is it worth it to sacrifice what you have for what you will become? Yes, it is. When you give up, you will go up. Trust God and you will see.

GROWTH ACTIVITIES

Mental preparation plays an important role in any achievement, especially one requiring sacrifice. As you consider the things you must give up in order to go up, you will find that the major challenge is surrendering them spiritually and psychologically. The things themselves hold little power over you. It is your desire for them, the fear of losing them, or the ego satisfaction you gain from them that make the sacrifice difficult. Here are growth activities that will help you identify and surrender the good that may be standing between you and God's best.

PRACTICE THE DISCIPLINE OF FASTING

Fasting may be the least practiced of all spiritual disciplines, despite the fact that Jesus both fasted and gave instruction on fasting. The neglect of this practice shows how averse we are to surrendering good things, for food is certainly a good thing. Fasting is a discipline of absence. When we fast, we subtract something from our lives in order to feel the want of it and allow that hunger to drive us closer to the Father. When you fast, you open a channel for the Holy Spirit to speak into your heart. It is one of the most powerful spiritual tools that we have.

Practice letting go by fasting for a period of time. If you are unfamiliar with this discipline, begin with just one meal. As you gain experience, you may extend your fast to a day or longer. Notice how constantly you think of food, especially in the beginning. Be aware of the time you spend preparing, eating, and cleaning up after meals. Allow your hunger to drive you to a deeper knowledge of yourself and a more intimate relationship with your heavenly Father. As you fast, ask the Holy Ghost to reveal to you any good thing that you should surrender in pursuit of God's best.

DOWNSIZE

We live in a culture of consumption and are barely aware of the abundance at our disposal. We lack little or nothing, for if we don't have an item in our home we can usually locate it at a nearby store and obtain it the same day. Again, all of these may be good things, but their very presence may hinder you from seeing the greater things that God has in mind for you.

Open yourself to the possibility of letting go of some good things by starting with a few of the many good things that you own but do not need or use. You might go through your closet and donate any clothing items you have not worn for one year, or give away an extra set of dishware. You could take an inventory of your garage and sell or donate any tools or sports equipment that you do not use. For a deeper exercise in letting go, consider parting with a major item, such as a car or home, that is larger than you need or more expensive than you can afford. As you part with these things of temporary value, ask the Lord to reveal any more significant items that you may need to surrender.

PRACTICE SECRECY

The spiritual practice of secrecy is abstaining from taking credit for good things you have done. In other words, it is doing good things in secret. The purpose of this exercise is to reveal the strength of your ego so that you can surrender to Christ at a deeper level. As you practice this discipline, you will become aware of the value you place on things like recognition, reputation, achievement, and praise. This will be good practice for surrendering things such as past achievement and personal ambition in order to grow into God's best for your life.

To practice secrecy, simply avoid taking credit for a good thing you have done, or do a good deed in a way that ensures no one will know that you are responsible. Some examples of this are anonymously donating money to a person in need, not correcting someone who mistakenly attributes a good idea that you thought of to a coworker, or doing household chores without asking to be thanked for it. A similar way to let go of your own need for attention or praise is to give that attention to others. You can do that by complimenting coworkers on their performance or spending time listening to someone who needs emotional support. By doing simple things such as these, you will begin to see larger ways in which good things like affirmation or acclaim may hinder you from reaching up for God's best.

This is the stopping point for many on their journey to full potential. Though they may have a great sense of purpose, good internal motivation, and the ability to think strategically, they cannot bring themselves to part with a relationship, comfort, or other good things in order to grow further. They approach this crossroad and, like the wealthy young man who met with Jesus, go away saddened because they realize the sacrifice it will take to go further.

Yet I believe better things are in store for you. I believe you have the heart to face this challenge and move through it, with the Spirit's help. Remember, the more difficult it is to surrender something to Christ, the greater will be your victory on the other side. God never calls us to sacrifice for the sake of sacrifice. Instead, he shows us the things we will have to be free from if we are to take hold of something better. As the writer of Hebrews urges, "let us lay aside every weight, and the sin which doth so easily beset us, and let us run with patience the race that is set before us, Looking unto Jesus the author and finisher of our faith; who for the joy that was set before him endured the cross, despising the shame, and is set down at the right hand of the throne of God" (Heb. 12:1–2).

ACTION ITEMS

1. Choose one or more of the growth activities from this chapter and plan when, where, and how you will do it.

2. With your Growth Team, review the provisions for the journey from the Before You Begin section of this book and talk about how you are making use of them.

3. With your growth team, discuss your future plans now that you have completed this book. Determine whether you will continue meeting, and if so, how you will support one another in your ongoing growth.

4. Spend a period of time in prayer, asking the Holy Spirit to reveal to you any good thing that you may be too attached to. Ask for the courage to surrender it.

5. Share Strategy No. 7: Sacrifice Good for Best with someone today.

BRIAN KINSEY

7

Completing Your Journey

Work out your own salvation with fear and trembling. For it is God which worketh in you both to will and to do of his good pleasure.
—*Philippians 2:12–13*

The starter's gun sounded at precisely 3:00 p.m. on October 20, 1968, and seventy-four runners representing forty-one nations leapt into action. It was the start of the Olympic marathon, the longest race of the Games of the XIX Olympiad in Mexico City. The days leading up to the event had been fraught with tension as South Africa was uninvited to participate after international protests of their practice of Apartheid. Only ten days before the start of games, the Mexican government had ordered the military to break up a student protest in Plaza de las Tres Culturas. Dozens were killed and over 1,000 arrested. Four days before the marathon, two American medalists caused a stir by raising black-gloved fists in protest during the award ceremony. Everyone hoped that the marathon, always a centerpiece of the games, would be free from controversy.

The 26.2-mile contest began without incident. However, as the race wore on, some athletes began to suffer the effects of Mexico City's high altitude, some 7,350 feet above sea level. Lungs burned and muscles cramped as the runners fought for position. As the pack approached mile twelve, not quite halfway, a group of runners jostled one another. John Stephen Akhwari, the lone athlete representing Tanzania at the 1968 games, was pushed to the ground, dislocating his knee and badly bruising his shoulder. The runners disappeared into the distance as Akhwari limped to his feet in obvious pain. All observers expected him to abandon the race. To finish, let alone compete for a place, would be all but impossible. It seemed that controversy might once again take center stage at the Olympics.

Yet Akhwari took one step, then another, and limped on; grimacing with each footfall, he continued along the course. By 6:25 p.m. the Olympic stadium was nearly empty. Mamo Wolde of Ethiopia had been first to cross the finish line more than an hour before. The medals had been awarded, the anthem played, and the crowd was filtering toward the exits. Then Akhwari appeared, the last runner to enter the stadium. As he hobbled around the 400-meter track toward the finish line, the few remaining spectators began to cheer and news reporters scrambled back to their places. Against all odds, he had finished the grueling contest, injured but undaunted, one hour and five minutes behind the winner.

When someone later asked Akhwari why he had chosen to fight through the pain and continue the race even though he had no hope of winning, the thirty-year-old athlete delivered the unrehearsed line that made him an international sensation and the hero of the 1968 games. He said, "My country did not send me 5,000 miles to start the race. They sent me 5,000 miles to finish it."[1]

You too, have begun a very long race, the journey to your full potential. There will be unexpected turns in your journey, just as there are for every long-distance runner. This process of growth may be longer and more grueling than you have anticipated. You may be jostled by circumstances, problems, or conflicts. You may face difficulties of many kinds, and you will certainly be tempted to abandon the race. In those moments, remember the example of John Stephen Akhwari—and remember that of the seventy-four runners who began that Olympic marathon, only fifty-seven completed it. There is little honor in beginning the race; there is great honor in completing it. Keep going. Do not become weary in your quest. You will grow as you keep applying the principles of this book to your life.

As you continue, here are three important things to keep in mind. Do them, and you will make good progress.

SHARPEN YOUR TOOLS

At the outset of this journey, we identified five provisions you would need to keep growing toward your full potential (see the Before You Begin section). These are not the growth principles themselves but are tools to put in your backpack to keep you going. They are:

- Purpose
- Hope

- Encouragement
- A Positive Attitude
- Determination

As you apply the growth principles to your life, sharpen these tools from time to time. Take them out of your backpack and put them to use. Think on them. Pray about them. Employ them frequently in your growth assessment and planning. Talk about them with your Growth Team. Do not allow these valuable resources to stay locked away in a drawer. Use them daily to keep you motivated and growing.

EXPECT GROWTH SPURTS AND DRY SPELLS

Every change curve has its peaks and valleys, and your growth to full potential will be no different. There will be times, perhaps like right now, when you are highly energized and begin to see good—even dramatic—progress. That is exciting, and you should celebrate it and share it with others. However, there is a valley on the other side of every mountaintop, and you should not be surprised to encounter times when the work is hard, growth is slow, and progress is negligible. Don't worry, and don't give up. At those times, learn to embrace the lessons that come from waiting. Keep working the seven growth principles into your life, and you will again see a season of good progress. Life is built on cycles, and your growth will have cycles too.

DON'T CLIMB ALONE

Finally, don't attempt this journey as a solo effort. Hopefully, you are already working with a Growth Team, a small group of likeminded people who will encourage you, hold you accountable, and help you to grow—and for whom you will provide those same helps. The surest way to become discouraged or distracted is to make this journey alone. You need your Growth Team. If your current team cannot stay together, find an accountability group, a growth partner, or a mastermind group that will help you keep growing. Together, you will go further and climb higher than you ever could alone.

Though the Games of the XIX Olympiad concluded decades ago, the story of John Stephen Akhwari has not been forgotten by the Olympic faithful. In 2008 he was a torchbearer in Dar es Salaam, Tanzania, when the Olympic torch relay made its way through his country, and that same year he was invited to Beijing as a goodwill ambassador in preparation for the Games of the XXIX Olympiad. His story wonderfully illustrates Paul's teaching that we must "not become weary in doing good, for at the proper time we will reap a harvest if we do not give up" (Gal. 6:9 NIV). Keep going, friend. I believe God has something wonderful in store for you as you grow to reach your full potential in Jesus Christ.

7

Notes

Before You Begin: Provisions for the Journey

1. David Crane, *Scott of the Antarctic: A Life of Courage, and Tragedy in the Extreme South* (London: HarperCollins, 2005), 398.

2. Megan Lane, "Four things Captain Scott found in Antarctica (and one that found him)," *BBC News Magazine*, November 2, 2011, http://www.bbc.com/news/magazine-15384729.

3. Leonard Huxley, ed., *Scott's Last Expedition, Volume I: Being the Journals of Captain R. F. Scott, R.N., C.V.O.* (London: Smith, Elder & Co., 1913), 572–573.

4. Ibid., 592.

5. Ibid., 595.

6. Oswald Chambers, "Impulsiveness or Discipleship," *My Utmost for His Highest: An Updated Edition in Today's Language*, (Grand Rapids, Mich.: Discovery House Publishers, 1992), entry for October 21.

7. John C. Maxwell, "The Right Picture of Success," *Leadership Wired Blog*, The John Maxwell Co., June 4, 2012, http://www.johnmaxwell.com/blog/the-right-picture-of-success.

Strategy No. 1: Discover Your Purpose

1. Harold Myra and Marshall Shelley, *The Leadership Secrets of Billy Graham* (Grand Rapids, Mich.: Zondervan, 2005), 72.

2. James C. Collins, *Good to Great: Why Some Companies Make the Leap—and Others Don't* (New York: HarperBusiness, 2001), 83–85.

3. "Table 1098. State Motor Vehicle Registrations, 1990 to 2009, Motorcycle Registrations and Licensed Drivers by State: 2009," U.S. Census Bureau, 2012, http://www.census.gov/compendia/statab/2012/tables/12s1098.pdf.

Strategy No. 3: Take Spiritual Authority

1. David R. Gergen, *Eyewitness to Power: The Essence of Leadership: Nixon to Clinton* (New York: Touchstone, 2000), 346.

2. John C. Maxwell, "The Laws of Personal Growth," *Leadership Wired Blog*, The John Maxwell Co., October 17, 2013, http://www.johnmaxwell.com/blog/the-laws-of-growth.

3. Becky Zerbe, "Penning a Marriage: The power of interactive journaling," *Today's Christian Woman*, September 2008, http://www.todayschristianwoman.com/articles/2008/september/7.22.html.

Strategy No. 4: Seek Divine Favor

1. As of July 21, 2015. "The Richest Person in Every State 2015: Warren Buffett," *Forbes.com*, http://www.forbes.com/profile/warren-buffett/.

2. Robert Smith, "Buffett Gift Sends $31 Billion to Gates Foundation," *NPR.com*, June 26, 2006, http://www.npr.org/templates/transcript/transcript.php?storyId=5512893.

3. Alex Crippen, "Buffett's gift to Gates Foundation is biggest ever," *CNBC.com*, July 15, 2014, Accessed June 2, 2015, http://www.cnbc.com/id/101838746.

4. "The Man with the Midas Touch," *MoneyControl.com*, http://www.moneycontrol.com/india/newsarticle/news_print.php?autono=256499&sr_no=1.

5. Stock price as of August 2014. "The Richest Person in Every State 2015," *Forebes.com*.

6. Larry Lea, *Wisdom: Don't Live Life Without It* (Nashville, Tenn.: Oliver-Nelson, 1990), 14.

7. "Ten Most Dangerous Intersections," Injury Board National News Desk, July 2, 2001, http://news.legalexaminer.com/view.cfm/news.legalexaminer.com/ten-most-dangerous.aspx?googleid=25238.

8. Mark Galli, *Jesus Mean and Wild: The Unexpected Love of an Untamable God*, (Grand Rapids, Mich.: Baker Books, 2006), 98–99.

9. Steven D. Levitt and Stephen J. Dubner, *Freakonomics: A Rogue Economist Explores the Hidden Side of Everything* (New York: William Morrow, 2005), 179–181.

10. Malcom Muggeridge, *Something Beautiful for God; Mother Teresa of Calcutta* (San Francisco: Harper & Row Publishers, 1971), 91–92.

Strategy No. 5: Learn from Pain

1. Open Doors USA, "Strong in the Storm," *Being Jesus' Disciple* (Torrance, Calif.: Rose Publishing Inc., 2010), 99.

2. Ibid.

3. Tom Friend, "How 'The Fridge' lost his way," *ESPN.com*, February 6, 2011, http://sports.espn.go.com/nfl/playoffs/2010/news/story?id=6091766.

4. "A story with some teeth: Fridge gets a new smile," *Chicago Tribune*, December 20, 2007, http://articles.chicagotribune.com/2007-12-20/sports/0712190874_1_teeth-new-smile-procedure.

5. C. S. Lewis, *The Problem of Pain* (New York: The MacMillan Company, 1948), 81.

6. Malcom Muggeridge, *A Twentieth-Century Testimony* (Nashville, Tenn.: Thomas Nelson, 1978), 19.

7. John MacArthur, "Joseph: Because God Meant It for Good," the website of *Grace to You*, April 29, 2012, http://www.gty.org/resources/sermons/80-388/joseph-because-god-meant-it-for-good.

8. A Methodist Preacher, *John Wesley the Methodist* (New York: The Methodist Book Concern, 1903) 298.

9. Corrie ten Boom, *The Hiding Place* (Peabody Mass.: Hendrickson Publishers, 2009), 240.

Strategy No. 6: Practice Strategic Thinking

1. Lewis Carroll, *The Complete Works of Lewis Carroll* (London: The Nonesuch Press, 1939), 64.

2. John C. Maxwell, *Thinking for a Change: 11 Ways Highly Successful People Approach Life and Work* (New York: Warner Books, 2003), 67.

3. Stephen R. Covey, *The Seven Habits of Highly Effective People: Restoring the Character Ethic* (New York: Free Press, 1989), 95.

4. Gina Shaw, reviewed by Laura J. Martin M.D., "Sleep Through the Decades: How sleep changes with age, once you're an adult," *WebMD*, http://www.webmd.com/sleep-disorders/features/adult-sleep-needs-and-habits.

5. Sun Tzu, *The Art of War,* trans. by Thomas Cleary, (Boston: Shambhala Publications, Inc., 1988), 56.

Strategy No. 7: Sacrifice Good for Best

1. This quote is widely circulated and often attributed to Charles Dubois. However, the saying more likely originates from the book *Approximations* (1922) by Charles Du Bos: *"Premier tressaillement vital; surtout il s'agit à tout moment de*

sacrifier ce que nous sommes à ce que nous pouvons devenir." "Charles Du Bos," *Wikipedia: the Free Encyclopedia*, https://en.wikipedia.org/wiki/Charles_Du_Bos.

2. Steve Mariboli, "Inspirational Quotes," the website of Steve Mariboli, http://www,stevemaraboli.com/Inspirational Quotes.html.

3. James C. Collins, *Good to Great: Why Some Companies Make the Leap—and Others Don't* (New York: HarperBusiness, 2001), 21.

Completing Your Journey

1. Stan Isaacs, "Bud's Olympiads Are Worth Their Weight in Gold" *Newsday* (November 5, 1991), 109.